THE GOOD COOK'S BOOK OF
Mustard

OTHER BOOKS BY MICHELE ANNA JORDAN

The Good Cook's Book of Oil & Vinegar
A Cook's Tour of Sonoma

THE GOOD COOK'S BOOK OF
Mustard

WITH MORE THAN 100 RECIPES

Michele Anna Jordan

Foreword by Madeleine Kamman
Illustrations by Michel Stong

▲
▼▼

ADDISON-WESLEY PUBLISHING COMPANY
Reading, Massachusetts   Menlo Park, California   New York
Don Mills, Ontario   Wokingham, England   Amsterdam   Bonn
Sydney   Singapore   Tokyo   Madrid   San Juan
Paris   Seoul   Milan   Mexico City   Taipei

Many of the designations used by manufacturers and sellers to distinguish their products are claimed as trademarks. Where those designations appear in this book and Addison-Wesley was aware of a trademark claim, the designations have been printed in initial capital letters.

Library of Congress Cataloging-in-Publication Data

Jordan, Michele Anna.
The good cook's book of mustard : with more than 100 recipes /
Michele Anna Jordan; foreword by Madeleine Kamman;
illustrations by Michel Stong.
p.   cm.
Includes bibliographical references and index.
ISBN 0-201-62257-2
1. Cookery (Mustard)   2. Mustard (Condiment)   I. Title.
TX819.M87J67 1994
641.6'384—dc20   93-33996
CIP

Cover and interior illustrations by Michel Stong
Cover design by Diana Coe
Text design by Karen Savary
Set in 11-point Weiss by Carol Woolverton

1 2 3 4 5 6 7 8 9-ARM-97969594
First printing, April 1994

*This book is dedicated
to the memory of my friend
Mary Frances Kennedy Fisher
1908—1992*

CONTENTS

RECIPES BY COURSE

FOREWORD

We tend to take our food for granted because we have to eat. So, we often eat without ever giving thanks to whichever deity we worship for our daily fare. Or then, tipping the scale way down in the opposite direction, some of us look at food, not as deserving of our full gratitude or to be enjoyed unconditionally, but as a part of a strict social rite to practice with business partners, or even, in extreme cases, as a way to climb the ladder of fame.

Mercifully there are also the others, all those who work in small communities, keeping the flame of good fare burning for all, using their fresh local ingredients with enthusiasm and personal flair, teaching the gospel of purity and simplicity. Michele Jordan is one of these dedicated souls. Long before she came to the School for American Chefs as my student, I noticed her well-written articles in a Sonoma County newspaper and admired her good culinary sense and techniques.

Michele has now written a very lively book on the liveliest of all condiments and my very favorite of all: the lowly mustard. May this attractive volume bring all cooks and inveterate cookbook readers a joyous renewed acquaintance with this oldest and most popular taste booster.

Madeleine Kamman
Director and Professor
School for American Chefs,
   Beringer Vineyards
St. Helena, Ca., October 1993

ACKNOWLEDGMENTS

Writing *The Good Cook's Book of Mustard* was a lonely affair, perhaps because I developed the recipes and completed the research during the months following the death of M. F. K. Fisher. As I worked alone in my kitchen or drove to the library at the University of California in Berkeley, I thought of her often, longed for the conversations we would no longer have. She was my nearly constant unseen companion during the months of testing and retesting, writing and rewriting, and this book is for her.

There are many people who contributed to the completion of this book and I offer them all a huge group hug of thanks and appreciation. Here I especially want to acknowledge my editor at Addison-Wesley, Elizabeth Carduff, for her sensitive and unwavering support for my work, for her always intelligent and essential advice, and for her vision of *The Good Cook's Book* series; her assistant, Len Gilbert, for never losing his sense of humor, at least not with me; Madeleine Kamman who shares her talent, sound advice and technical knowledge with elegant generosity; my agents Angela Miller, for loving my recipes and saying so with such enthusiasm, and Betsy Amster, for the emergency ride to the airport; my wonderful assistants, Betty Ellsworth and Lesa Tanner, without whom I would be thoroughly lost; my good friends John Boland, publisher, and Jim Carroll, editor, of *The Sonoma County Independent*, who keep me in Sonoma County in spite of my growing wanderlust; Barry Levenson of the Mount Horeb Mustard Museum, a generous and entertaining resource; Anna Cherney, who celebrates her 93rd birthday this year, for her generous support and faith in my work; and to the meticulous Leisel Hoffman for her enormous assistance with the copyediting.

I also want to acknowledge my growing New York family: Elizabeth Knowles, Jim Spencer, Ann Halcomb, Chris Carduff, Joe Caldwell, Patty Wieman, Craig Pomranz, Tom Fernandez, and Fred Kinnard. Special thanks, too, to the Corporation of Yaddo.

Finally, a warm, loving thank you to my Sonoma County friends and family, especially my daughters Gina and Nicolle, Ginny Stanford, Jerry and Patty Hertz, Guy and Mary Duryee, Rob Cole, Leslie Janik, Julieta Leal Weiss, State Senator Mike Thompson, Lou Preston and Linda Villagomez of Preston Vineyards and Winery, Steve Gardner of KSRO-AM, Jon Stong, and with continued admiration for her beautiful, evocative contributions to my books and my life, artist Michel Stong.

INTRODUCTION

I

In March of 1993, I was on the train headed north from New York City to Saratoga Springs, and from there to Yaddo, the artists' colony on the outskirts of town. A few days earlier, I had left California's Sonoma County in the full bud of spring, its greens and golds and yellows stretched out over the countryside that I had loved and thrived in for over two decades. As I rode through the stark gray Hudson River Valley, the earth was wrapped in a monotone dream, nothing but the soft, uniform colors of winter in the Northeast, a sight entirely new to this born-and-bred California girl. The journey became a barren dreamscape between youthful California and the enduring splendor of Yaddo, a magical piece of land already alive with creative energy when my homeland was still in the early struggles of new statehood. In 1849, a year before California became a state, Edgar Allan Poe composed *The Raven* on the site that was to become Yaddo.

For two months, I would neither cook nor test a recipe nor wander through gourmet shops looking for inspiration among the wines and the oils, the vinegars and the honeys, the mustards. I would not visit a farm market, nor would I gather armfuls of wild spring mustard for my table. Rather, I would spend my days and nights writing and reading and reflecting in the protected solitude that only an artists' colony can provide. I would work on a project about my friend and mentor, M. F. K. Fisher. As I anticipated the weeks ahead, and of time spent immersing myself in her work and of mingling my voice with hers, I thought of some of our last days together and of a particular visit nearly a year earlier, in the last spring of her life.

In that spring of 1992, California was in its sixth year of drought. January was dry; February brought no rain; in March each day was bright and harsh. Thirst prevailed in all of us and in everything: in the fields and hills that were the dry gold of summer already, in the deer who came down toward the towns and cities to find food and water, in the streams and creeks that had slowed to a trickle or less. We were very thirsty. And then in early April, the rains at last came, glorious torrents that drenched the thirsty soil, germinating seeds that had long lain dormant. The rains were not enough to ease the drought; those would come the next year. But they were sufficient to awaken the sleeping mustard, a hearty seed that can drowse within the soil for a hundred years, awaiting the proper conditions.

The mustard that bloomed soon after was the most beautiful, most abundant any of us had seen in years, perhaps decades. Every piece of undeveloped land seemed covered in a bright yellow fever. Mustard was woven between grapevines like gold stitches on a patchwork quilt; it stretched over the vast open spaces between the towns and cities of Sonoma County; it covered the low, lush hills of Alexander Valley in a profusion of golden blossoms. The hearty yellow flowers pushed through cracks in sidewalks and cement. It was a glorious, dizzying display, and it was through this golden turmoil that I drove to see my friend.

With her vocal cords ravaged by illness, Mary Frances could no longer converse, so during my visits I often read to her. To capture the spirit of this warm day with its mustard covering the hills around us, I had brought along a story I had written called "Mustard Love," about my first spring in Sonoma County, when I lived in the low hills east of the town of Petaluma in an area known as Lakeville and drove daily through the back roads to the university where I was a student. There were no housing developments in Lakeville at that time, no shopping centers or luxury homes; there was, in fact, nothing much at all except eucalyptus trees and sweeping, gilded fields of mustard, nearly heartbreaking in their beauty. It reminded me of a train ride between Paris and Épernay, where for mile after mile as far as the eye could see there had been nothing but golden mustard and the sharp blue sky.

Mary Frances apparently enjoyed the piece, smiling and shrugging her shoulders in a characteristically evocative gesture that always seemed to convey pleasure. We talked of Dijon, and of the intriguing black facade of the Grey Poupon store on the corner of rue de la Liberté where we had both bought mustard. After our visit, as I wound my way back through the yellow hills to my home in Sebastopol, *The Good Cook's Book of Mustard* sprung to mind, fully formed and in clear focus. Once its publication was secured, I told Mary Frances of the project, of how I conceived of it that day with her when we read the mustard story, of how together we had evoked so vividly my memories of France in the spring and the tastes and smells of Dijon. The book was clearly hers, I said, as the dedication would show. Beyond words at all by that time, she gripped my hand, hunched up her shoulders, and beamed for a minute. I felt she approved and was pleased, even though she often criticized single-subject cookbooks. I kissed her hand and, for the first time in her presence, had to hold back tears. She died just a few days later, on June 22, 1992. I hope this book tells a story that would make her proud to appear on its first pages.

II

Although this book began as both a simple labor of love and an exploration of a favorite ingredient, it quickly became an exercise in fun and good humor as well. There is something about mustard that makes people act, well, silly. During the year or so that I worked on the manuscript, I came across inane recipes, goofy T-shirts, buttons shouting *Please Pass the Mustard,* and even a silent film from the 1920s complete with a mock trial of a gentleman ignorant enough to try to eat a ham sandwich without mustard. The sandwich, represented by a skilled and wonderfully costumed actor, offered crucial evidence. Before too long, my trail led me to the court jester of mustard humor, Barry Levenson, and his Mount Horeb Mustard Museum in Mount Horeb, Wisconsin.

The discovery of Barry and his passion was like tapping into a great golden vein of subterranean mustard. Barry loves mustard, collects it, writes about it, and sells it. He epitomizes the lighthearted exuberance, the robust silliness, and expansive good humor with which mustard lovers pursue their hearts' desire.

Barry's food emporium offers scores of commercial mustards that I have not seen elsewhere. I decided to try a selection of his favorites. The box arrived by second-day air and I set out with every intention of being judicious and measured in my tasting, trying three or four, writing for a while, sampling again, so that my palate would be fresh and open for each new round. About thirty minutes later, I was happily lost in a golden fog, dozens of mustard jars open around me, spoons everywhere, all of my mineral water gone, cracker crumbs scattered like confetti testifying to my frenzied feast. One particular jar sat empty, a Vidalia onion mustard that is without doubt the best commercial mustard condiment I have ever tasted. I took a deep breath and settled back to recover.

Mustard at its best is like that, conducive of harmless indulgence and lusty good times. It is with this spirit that I suggest you approach finding your favorite mustard condiments—with enthusiasm informed by the hints and guidelines I offer throughout this book. I wish you as much of a good time as I had, and as I continue to have as new mustards appear on the market almost weekly.

Finally, I couldn't possibly write about one of my favorite foods without allowing myself to indulge in touting my specific preferences. This is not an objective assessment, but rather a highly opinionated tribute to the mustards I like best of all. *The Good Cook's Book of Mustard* is not really about commercial mustards or about condiments made with the spice. It is about *mustard* itself, its many varieties and preparations, its history and early uses, the folklore that attributes specific powers to it, and the many ways it functions in the kitchen. Still, when we cook with mustard, we must choose from among the hundreds that line our market shelves. I'm happy to share the ones that I prefer.

My favorite brand of mustard at the moment is a sassy little Dijon from the French company *PIC*, imported exclusively by a store in Berkeley, California, Kermit Lynch Wine Merchant, which also imports some of Italy's finest olive oils and great French and Italian wines. The mustard is irresistibly good and I'm forever sneaking fingerfuls of it as I walk past one of several mustard shelves in my kitchen. I like it so much I buy it by the case. When making, say, mustard cream, I notice a significant difference when I use *PIC*. It is the most suave, elegant mustard I have come across.

After *PIC*, I favor *Dessaux* and *L'Étoile* for Dijon mustards, and when I can't find those, Grey Poupon serves me well. I often hear Grey Poupon Dijon mustard, now made domestically by Nabisco Foods, Inc., criticized and I heartily disagree. Licensed by Grey Poupon of France to produce the only Dijon mustard outside of France, Nabisco does an outstanding job. The texture is perfect and if it's not quite as strong as the French-made Grey Poupon, it still packs a good wallop of heat. The flavors are well balanced, and it is not overly salty. Grey Poupon is one of the few excellent ingredients that one can find in nearly every supermarket. And it is relatively inexpensive, so don't break your budget looking for the most exotic Dijon mustard around. Good Dijon mustard from French producers is often a treat, and I pick up new ones when I see them. But for day-to-day cooking, when I need mustard for a sauce or a soup, I know that I will get consistently good, reliable flavor with Grey Poupon. Maille, a French company older than Grey Poupon, makes an excellent Dijon, as well as a green peppercorn mustard that has a superb flavor, although I don't like the fact that it contains vegetable oil.

I don't care for most of the Dijon-style mustards made in this country, either by major companies or by small producers. I wish I could say otherwise, but I can't. I find they have a floury texture and lack both the compelling goodness of my favorites and the elegance of the French mustards. There are, however, scores of wonderful flavored mustards made by small companies all over the country, many of which begin with a commercial mustard base that is most often imported. I am wild about the Vidalia onion mustard made by Oak Hill Farms in Atlanta, Georgia; Duck Puddle Farm of Ivyland, Pennsylvania, makes a fine Southwestern mesquite mustard that is great with smoked poultry (or by the spoonful). A lovely whole-grain mustard is made by Arran Provisions on the Isle of Arran, Scotland; and I love the dark richness of the black mustard made by Wilson's of Essex, England.

And finally, a hot dog on the street in New York City, San Francisco, Santa Rosa, anywhere at all, should be topped with any humble ballpark mustard, sharp and bright and perfectly suited to its purpose.

PART ONE

All About Mustard

WHAT IS MUSTARD?

A friend opens his desk drawer and there sits a tiny plastic package, one side white, the other clear, revealing the bright yellow mixture inside: ballpark or *American* mustard, a remnant of a now forgotten lunch on the run, a sandwich at his desk, perhaps, or egg rolls from the nearby Thai restaurant, which are always accompanied by the little packets. This is a scene repeated across the country daily, people finding little packages full of mustard when they open their desk drawers, their cars' glove compartments, the packets of silverware and condiments on airlines, a bag holding a deli sandwich or some Chinese-to-go. Millions of little packages of mustard spurt their yellow interiors each year; millions more are discarded, forgotten, tossed into the corner of the pantry. Ask an American child about mustard and chances are the description will closely resemble the sharp yellow paste inside the little packet my friend found. This is mustard as most Americans have known it in this century, the mustard M. F. K. Fisher described as tasting "bright yellow," a flavor she considered essential to her chilled buttermilk soup. It is, indeed, *our* mustard, but it is not mustard as most of the world has known it or knows it today.

Mustard is a plant, a member of the *Brassica* genus of the *Cruciferae* family, so named for its flowers, which sport four petals in a crosslike configuration. All varieties of mustard are fast growing and, like other *brassicas*, thrive in cooler weather. Mustard blooms in the early spring and, in many areas, its bright yellow flowers are the first sign of the coming of the new season. Each mustard plant produces hundreds of seeds that are grouped together in pods. Today, commercial mustard seed comes from just three species of *Brassica*, but the seeds of mustard plants, both wild and cultivated, have been used for millennia to season the foods we eat. In earliest times, the seeds were chewed with meat, possibly to disguise the flavor of decay. There are records of mustard's cultivation as early as 5000 to 4000 B.C., and mustard seeds have been found in Egypt's great pyramids. In A.D. 42, Columella's *De re rustica* included a recipe similar to today's well-known mustard sauce, which is simply a mixture of ground mustard seed, acidic liquid, and seasonings. Although technically, *mustard* can refer to the entire plant, it is prepared mustard, this sauce with such ancient roots, that we think of when we hear the word. What is it, exactly, that has intrigued the human palate for so many thousands of years?

The characteristic quality of mustard is its sharp, bright heat, an element that is released partially by the simple chewing of the raw seed. This sensation is the result of a chemical reaction that occurs when the outer shell, or husk, of the mustard seed is shattered and its cellular structure broken. The enzyme myrosin, in the presence of oxygen and water, reacts with a glucoside within the seed's heart to produce a particularly volatile substance, acrinyl isothiocyanate in white mustard and allyl isothiocyanate in brown and black mustards. With white mustard, the burning sensation caused by this compound is felt only on the tongue. With brown and black mustards, there is also a sense of vaporization that affects the eyes, nose, and sinuses in much the same way as with the Japanese horseradish *wasabi*. This sensation is activated by the same chemical, the glucoside sinigrin, in each. The reaction is both the key to mustard's intrigue and the reason mustard was not widely accepted in the United States until 1904, when Francis French developed a mild recipe based exclusively on white mustard seeds. He suspected that Americans were not buying mustard because they did not like its heat, and his success suggests that he was right. Today, French's mustard—bright yellow from turmeric and tart from vinegar—accounts for 40 percent of all mustard consumed in this country. The rest of the world, however, seems to prefer mustard not only with more heat, but also with more nuance and range of flavor.

Mustard's many nuances come not so much from its natural flavors, but from the ingredients used to produce the mustard paste or sauce. There is limited variation in mustard itself: mild and hot, and coarse-ground or smooth. It is the choice of liquids, of flavoring agents, and the degree of milling that determines the subtle variations in a particular mustard's taste and texture. A variety of liquids—from apple cider vinegar and lemon juice to wine and beer—may contribute their flavors, and a broad range of herbs, spices, and aromatics add essential elements. Nearly all mustards are, and should be, finished with the addition of salt, which not only helps preserve the flavors, but, because salt melts slowly on the tongue, also brings them together in a harmonious finish on the palate.

Although it is mustard the sauce, mustard the condiment, that we think of when we hear *mustard*, the word also refers to the dry ground seeds, many types of greens, and, in regional slang, to the delicious yellow fat in the center of a crab's body. What you receive when you ask for "the mustard" varies greatly with where you do the asking. Certainly, if you're standing at the elbow of a crab picker in Maryland, you just might get that delicious fat. In many regions of France, you would be given a pot of Dijon, though in certain areas you might receive a tart, coarse-grained mixture, the mustard of Bordeaux or of Meaux. In America's heartland and in diners nearly everywhere, you would receive a plastic squeeze bottle of the bright yellow sauce. In restaurants in cities like Berkeley, San Francisco, Boston, Chicago, and New York, however, you would receive a more fashionable mixture, probably a Dijon, but possibly a housemade specialty mustard. In delicatessens, your options might be limited to American brown mustard, a mildly spicy mustard that is less tart than ballpark mustard. In Chinese restaurants throughout North America, a small bowl of very hot mustard, a simple mix of water and hot mustard flour, would be set on your table. In Germany, the mixture might be coarse or smooth, but in either case it would probably be brown rather than yellow, somewhat sweet, and fairly hot. In England, it would depend on where you were, although in most places you probably wouldn't have to ask for mustard. It is automatically served with roast beef, bangers, Cheddar cheese, and other standard British fare. Many pubs feature their own house blends, and the English are known for their hot mustards.

Interestingly, mustard as a condiment seems to be most popular in northern temperate climates. It is not widely used in Latin America (although it is popular in Argentina, where beef is a major part of the diet) nor in most of Africa. The Arab world has largely ignored mustard. India uses mustard oil and mustard seed, but prepared mustard is not among the many condiments that accompany most Indian meals. With limited exceptions, mustard does not play a significant role in the cuisines of southern Europe either.

CUTTING THE MUSTARD *The phrase "cut the mustard" is a common contemporary expression, indicating that someone is up to the task or the standards at hand. According to the 1986 edition of* The Dictionary of American Slang, *it entered the English language in the early 1900s from Philadelphia, where it was said that "groups . . . have special vested interests. And that's not gonna cut the mustard." It is suggested that mustard refers to "the genuine thing" and may be based on mustard as hot, keen, and sharp, all of which can also mean excellent.*

An endless field of bright yellow mustard stretching as far as the eye can see is a glorious sight and one that is repeated throughout the world each spring. Mustard thrives in any temperate climate and requires no special care to grow. Rather the opposite, actually; so prolific and hardy is the plant that it is often considered a weed. Mustard, however brilliant in the spring, is commonplace. Although it is the world's second most popular spice—only black pepper is consumed in greater quantity—no wars have been fought to obtain it and it has never commanded a high price on the world market.

Mustard, the plant, received its common name from the prepared condiment *mustum*, referring to the unsweetened, unfermented grape juice with which it was blended by the Romans, and *ardens*, referring to its fiery taste. Although just three species of the genus *Brassica* are harvested to produce what we generally call mustard, the word itself sometimes is used to indicate all *brassicas*, making such diverse vegetables as broccoli, cabbages, bok choy, Brussels sprouts, cauliflower, kale, kohlrabi, rutabaga, and turnip seem more closely related than they actually are. They are indeed part of the same family, *Cruciferae*, and of the same genus, *Brassica*, but they belong to different species entirely. All *brassicas* display the four-petaled flowers of their family, all are fast growing, and all flourish in cooler weather. Most members of the large group also contain chemicals that, in the presence of oxygen, precipitate a reaction that creates a volatile, irritating oil, but in many members, it is released primarily as an aroma rather than as a sensation on the palate. Only a few member plants produce the sort of heat given off by mustard.

Humans have taken advantage of mustard's savory qualities for thousands of years, and because its use extends far back into prehistory, it is impossible to know its exact origins with certainty. There are indications that mustard seeds were chewed by our ancestors as long as ten thousand years ago. These seeds would have been gathered from wild mustard. Records indicate that mustard was cultivated in China four or five thousand years before the birth of Christ. White mustard heralds from the eastern Mediterranean. Black mustard was first recorded in Persia, and brown mustard had its genesis in the Himalayan region, although the plant appears to have migrated to three separate regions— China, the southern Ukraine, and the Indian subcontinent (India, Pakistan, and Bangladesh)—where it developed distinct and different characteristics. Although today the majority of mustard worldwide is made from the seeds of *Brassica juncea*, the variety that developed in Bangladesh was unsuitable for this purpose. Its seeds were—and are—used for their mustard oil.

Romans took the mustard seed with them to Gaul, thus introducing what would become a spice strongly identified with France and French cuisine. Dijon, ancient capital of Burgundy in eastern France, today is considered the capital of the mustard world. Indeed, its very name is synonymous with the prepared condiment and over half of the world's prepared mustard comes from Dijon. From France, the use of mustard spread throughout Europe, into England, and to America with the first Spanish explorers. It grows

wild throughout North America, although it is generally believed that Spanish padres scattered it along the Pacific Coast, where it flourishes today. Upon his return to America after serving as minister to France, Thomas Jefferson planted mustard in his garden and ordered the prepared condiment from Paris. Mustard naturalizes quickly—that is, it reseeds itself and needs no human intervention to thrive—and by the time of the Civil War, some seventy years after Jefferson's planting, there were plenty of greens from the wild mustard in the region to provide essential nourishment for the soldiers.

Today, mustard grows wild in every temperate region of the world. It is cultivated in many countries, but Canada supplies the majority of the world's commercial mustard needs. Additionally, commercial farmers and home gardeners grow dozens of types of mustards. It is a robust, fast-growing plant whose leaves make an excellent green for both salads and sautéing. Some varieties have a great deal of heat, even when they are quite young; others are milder, with just a hint of mustard's characteristic fire. Mustard sprouts also provide an interesting, easy way to introduce mustard's spicy flavor into our diets. They can be grown on any kitchen counter, and can be used whenever more common sprouts—alfalfa or onion, for example—are called for. They are particularly good on chicken sandwiches and on simple cream cheese sandwiches, where they add a bright spark of flavor.

HOW TO GROW MUSTARD SPROUTS **Soak 2 or 3 tablespoons of white or brown mustard seeds in water overnight. Wet a tea towel thoroughly with water and wring it out so that it is still fairly wet but not dripping. Fold it and place it in an oblong glass baking dish (9 by 6 inches is an ideal size). Drain the seeds and spread them over the surface of the towel, between the folds. Keep the seeds in a warm (but not hot) place for 3 or 4 days, misting them regularly with enough water to keep them moist. By the fourth, or possibly the fifth, day they should be about 1½ inches long and ready to harvest. Refrigerate them in a sealed container and use them within 2 or 3 days.**

Mustard's agricultural importance stretches beyond its use as a food crop. It functions as green manure when it is plowed back into the earth before it goes to seed. Mustard

VARIETIES OF LEAF MUSTARD
BRASSICA JUNCEA

These mustards represent the nonhybrid seed currently available in the United States.

VARIETY	OTHER NAMES	DESCRIPTION
Aka Takana	India mustard	Large dark purple leaves with white ribs; pungent
Ao Takana	India mustard	Large bright green leaves; pungent
Common Leaved Curled	Chinese Leaf mustard new in 1987	Dwarf with thick stems
Dai Gai Choi	Broadleaf Mustard Cabbage	Tall, large green leaves, broad stems; closed heads; mustard flavor
Florida Broad Leaf	Large Smooth Leaf	Round or oval serrated dark green leaves, cream-colored ribs
Florida Giant	new in 1991	
Fordhook Fancy	Burpee's Fordhook Fancy	Fringed deeply curled dark green leaves; mild
Gai Choi	Chinese Mustard Cabbage, Chinese Mustard Spinach, India mustard	Tall; mild but distinct mustard flavor
Giant Curled		Deep green leaves, crimped and frilled at edges; mild
Giant Curled Chinese	India mustard	Bright green curly leaves; excellent as cooked greens or in salads

VARIETY	OTHER NAMES	DESCRIPTION
Giant Red	Japanese mustard	Large deep purplish red leaves with white ribs; strong mustard flavor
Giant Southern Curled		Large bright green leaves, curled and fringed on edges
Green Wave	Yellow/Green Curly; Chinese Green Wave	Darkest green of curly mustards; spineless, deeply frilled; spicy hot flavor
Green in Snow		From northern China; mild flavor; good in winter greenhouses, early spring, late fall
India mustard		Semiclosed head, large leaves on broad thick stems; lots of mustard taste
Leaf Heading	Chinese Leaf mustard	Large light green leaves; sweet and tender
Miike Giant	Giant Japanese Tendergreen	Thick dark green leaves, crumpled and frilled; pungent
Miike Purple	Japanese mustard	Purple, clear peppery taste
Old Fashion	Old Fashion Ragged Edge mustard; Hen Peck	Long, ruffled leaves; superb for salads
Slobolt	new in 1987	Smooth, dark green leaves
Southern Giant Curled	Southern Curled	Large, bright green leaves with crumpled frilled edges; mild, mustardy flavor

Source: *Garden Seed Inventory*, 3rd edition, 1992.

plants also attract garden pests. Harmful insects are drawn to their volatile oils and lay their eggs on the leaves. The mustard plants are then removed, the unhatched eggs along with them, before the pests can harm the crops. Mustard is particularly effective in attracting insects away from cabbage, cauliflower, radish, kohlrabi, Brussels sprouts, turnips, and collard greens. It is often planted between rows of fruit trees and grapevines where it will also draw insects from the crops, but commercial gardeners warn that it should be used with care and removed before it goes to seed. Mustard naturalizes in a single generation and, because its seed is so hardy, it can become an annoying weed. Wild mustard can be effectively broken, and thus controlled, by rolling a field—a technique common in farming—early in the day, while the mustard is still wet from the morning's dew. The secretions of mustard's roots help balance an acid soil, and although the white and black varieties are said to reduce populations of nematodes (parasitic worms found in some soils), they also deplete nonacid soil.

THE FAITH OF A SEED

The kingdom of heaven is like to a grain of mustard seed, which a man took, and sowed in his field: Which indeed is the least of all seeds: but when it is grown, it is the greatest among herbs, and becometh a tree, so that the birds of the air come and lodge in the branches thereof.

The Bible, New Testament, Matthew

How many, say, potatoes does it take to make a pound? Two, perhaps three, if you consider russets, or a dozen or so if you use small new red potatoes or Yellow Finns. How many tomatoes? Three, four, five, fifteen, depending on their type and size. A pound of cherries makes a good bagful, too many to eat in one sitting, except at the start of the season when no one can get enough. Anyone who shops can imagine a pound of almost anything: a dozen and a half thin stalks of asparagus, enough dry spaghetti to fit comfortably in one hand, four sticks of butter, a substantial chunk of cheese.

Now, try this: Imagine a pound of mustard seed. How many tiny yellow seeds, just three millimeters in diameter, does it take to make a handful, a cup, a full pound? One pound of white mustard seed—the largest of the three types of seed—contains approximately 70,000 seeds, or 4,375 seeds per ounce. Just one of those seeds can produce several hundred new seeds during its growing cycle. One begins to understand why mustard seed has been used throughout history as a symbol of fertility.

The Hindu religion in particular identifies the seed as a symbol of fecundity. Early Christians, too, looked to the seed's symbolic possibilities, but used it to express other aspects of their tradition. There are numerous biblical references to the tiny, resilient seed, most of which refer to its size and endurance. All the faith that one needs, Christians read, is as much as a grain of mustard seed. No doubt the seed was chosen in part because of its astonishing endurance, its innate ability to survive and transcend unfavorable conditions, waiting patiently in the ground until the rain comes in proper amounts and at the right time. Mustard can wait for decades, for as long as a hundred years or more, before sprouting. A mustard seed is full of remarkable power: all of mustard's potential—not just of the plant itself, but its heat and flavor—is contained within the small seed, a tiny miracle of which we avail ourselves with each squirt or spread or bite of mustard. It is no surprise that it has earned a place not only in our culinary history but in world mythology as well.

It is the outer shell, or husk, of the mustard seed that gives it its strength. A tough coating protects the interior heart and gives the seed the color by which it is known. What is called white mustard, *Brassica alba*, is actually a pale tan or pale yellow, frequently with the slightest blush of rose. *Brassica juncea* is known as brown mustard, and its seed is often a deep, rosy brown, although it can be nearly black. To confuse the matter, there is a yellow variety of this brown mustard, which is called, in the commercial mustard industry, oriental mustard. Black mustard, *Brassica nigra*, is close to the same size as brown mustard, and its color is a rosy brown rather than a true black. The seed itself is oval rather than round. Today, black mustard plays no significant role in the world mustard market. It is not grown commercially in North America and is cultivated in only a few places in the rest of the world. The seedpods of this mustard shatter easily, thus requiring it to be carefully harvested by hand. It is not profitable to grow mustard on a large scale in this manner, particularly when brown and oriental mustards have such similar qualities that even experts can be fooled.

Mustard's hard husk must be broken for mustard to sprout or release its flavor and heat. In the ground, or under a damp cloth in your kitchen, the interior of the seed absorbs water until the heart swells enough to burst open the shell and the tiny sprout begins to grow. A taste of a mustard sprout provides the full impact of mustard's heat.

Inside the mustard seed, the heart is made up of the endosperm and the bran. The mustard flour, or dry mustard, that most of us have seen is the endosperm ground to a fine powder, with the husk and bran sifted out. All mustard flour, once these other elements are removed, is yellow, although brown and oriental mustards are yellower than both yellow and white mustards. It is this mustard flour that is available to the home cook. Whole mustard seeds, crushed and sold as ground mustard, are available to the commercial food industry. Some of the ground mustard is used in salad dressings and sauces, but most goes into sausages and other prepared meat products. In all these products, it is used not only for the flavor it imparts but also for its binding and emulsifying abilities. It is mustard's bran that is primarily responsible for its ability to bind a sauce, although the mustard flour itself absorbs twice its weight in water and one and a half times its weight in oil, so it too helps thicken a mixture such as a vinaigrette or a sauce.

Today, much of the world's mustard seed is grown on the Canadian plains, where the hot, dry summer offers the best environment for the maturing and harvesting of the seed, which is cut by a combine. The northern plains of the United States also produce commercial mustard crops, but not nearly enough to supply even national demand for the seed. The United States is the second major importer of Canadian mustard, purchasing the majority of Canada's white mustard seed crop. France, where little commercial mustard is grown today, buys the largest quantity, purchasing primarily Canadian brown mustard.

TYPES OF MUSTARD SEED, THEIR HISTORY, AND THEIR USES

SCIENTIFIC NAME	*Brassica hirta*	*Brassica juncea*	*Brassica nigra*
COMMON NAME	White	Brown	Black
OTHER NAMES	*Sinapis alba;* *Brassica alba;* Yellow	Black, Oriental, Asian, Indian	*Sinapis nigra;* Brown
PLACE OF ORIGIN	Eastern Mediterranean	Himalayas	Persia (Iran)
CURRENT CULTIVATION	North America, England, Europe	North America, England, Europe, Russia	India, Nepal, Sicily, Ethiopia
COLOR OF HUSK	Pale tan to pale yellow	Yellow; brown to dark brown or black	Dark; purplish brown with red tones
CHARACTERISTICS	Largest seed; round; mildest heat felt only on tongue	Medium seed; round; intense heat felt on tongue and in eyes, nose, sinuses	Smallest seed; oval; difficult to harvest; intense heat felt on tongue and in eyes, nose, sinuses
ACTIVE CHEMICAL AGENTS	Myrosin reacts with sinalbin to produce acrinyl isothiocyanate	Myrosin reacts with sinigrin to produce allyl isothiocyanate	Myrosin reacts with sinigrin to produce allyl isothiocyanate
HISTORICAL USES	English dry; Alsace; Lorraine	Mustard oil; Dijon; Bordeaux, Meaux; other European	English dry; Dijon; Bordeaux, Meaux; other European

(cont'd)	Brassica hirta	Brassica juncea	Brassica nigra
CURRENT USES	Ballpark; English dry; mild mustard flour (retail); sprouts; ground mustard used in commercially processed meats	Mustard oil; English dry; Chinese style; Dijon and most other French and European; hot mustard flour (retail); sprouts	Limited because of difficulty of cultivation and harvest
GREENS USED	As cover crops and green manure; gathered wild in spring	Commercial mustard greens	Gathered wild in spring
RETAIL AVAILABILITY	Whole seeds; mustard flour; prepared	Whole seeds; mustard flour; prepared; greens; oil	Virtually unavailable

THE HISTORY OF A CONDIMENT

Clean the mustard seed very carefully. Sift it well and wash in cold water. After it is clean, soak it in cold water two hours. Stir it, squeeze it, and put into a new, or very clean, mortar. Crush it with a pestle. When it is well ground, put the resulting paste in the centre of the mortar, press and flatten it with the hand. Make furrows in the surface and put hot coals in them. Pour water with saltpetre over these. This will take the bitterness out of the seed and prevent it from moulding. Pour off the moisture completely. Pour strong white vinegar over the mustard, mix it thoroughly with the pestle, and force through a sieve.

Columella, *De re rustica*, A.D. 42

17

IF YOU COLLECT US, THEY WILL COME *In October of 1986, Barry Levenson was depressed. The Red Sox had just lost the World Series and Barry soothed himself by wandering the aisles of a twenty-four-hour supermarket. I need a hobby, he thought to himself in the 3:00 A.M. darkness, and when he passed the mustard section, Mount Horeb Mustard Museum folklore tells us he had a vision. "If you collect us, they will come," he heard, whispered perhaps by a spunky little jar of mustard longing for the limelight. He spent the thirteen dollars or so he had in his pocket and thus began what has become the world's largest collection of prepared mustards.*

At that time, Barry was an assistant attorney general for the state of Wisconsin, working in the criminal appeals division. He continued his dual existence, prosecutor by day, mustard collector by night, until 1991, when he resigned his full-time career position to work on his mustard collection and write screenplays.

In 1989, Barry opened the Mount Horeb Mustard Museum; in April 1992, the museum was moved to its current location in what has to be one of the grandest openings in history. Standing at the door of the new location, Barry turned to his wife, Pat, with that immortal request, "Please pass the mustard." She turned and repeated the request, and on and on it went through the line of over three hundred mustard fanatics braving a rainstorm to assist in the historic passing of the final jar of the mustard collection from the old museum to the new. When the request reached the old museum, associate curator Judy LeMasters started the plastic twenty-four-ounce squeeze jar of Plochman's yellow mustard toward its new home, while the mustard passers chanted, "Mustard si, mayo no!" and several rhymes celebrating the world's most popular condiment.

In addition to being museum curator and editor of its newsletter, The Proper Mustard, Barry Levenson is a mustard maker. He began with a single type, a cinnamon-honey mustard made with prepared Dijon, and he gave it as gifts to his friends. Everyone loved it. Barry had a label made and then decided he should have a line of products, three mustards under the brand Slimm & Nunne, since, he says, those are your chances of finding a better mustard. He added Golden Ginger Mustard and Kerala Curry Mustard, and finally decided he should make a mustard from scratch. He began with whole seeds, added beer, malt vinegar, and spices, and gave the world Slimm & Nunne's Grainy Gusto Mustard. Slimm & Nunne also launched what may be the world's only numbered, limited edition mustard, Grainy Gusto made with Garten Brau dark beer from Capital Brewery of Middleton, Wisconsin. In spring 1993, John Wagner & Sons took over production and distribution of Barry's mustard, renaming it Mount Horeb Mustard Museum Mustard.

Today, the mustard collection at the museum continues to grow, and at last count the number was approaching two thousand.

There is no question that it was the French who both perfected and popularized the preparation of mustard as a condiment. Although recipes for a paste similar to modern mustard appear as early as A.D. 42, the use of mustard as a condiment was not widely practiced in either Greece or Rome. The Romans introduced the seed to eastern Gaul in the region now known as *Bourgogne*, or Burgundy, with its well-known capital of Dijon, and from there it spread throughout western Europe. As early as the ninth century, French monasteries were bringing in considerable income from their mustard preparations. Although accounts of the development of the use of mustard in France are contradictory, records exist that allow us to assemble at least a skeleton of mustard's rise to prominence as the world's most popular condiment. With our imagination, we can add the flesh, the sinew, the heartbeat, and the blood. There is no dearth of detail, however anecdotal, to inspire us. Alexandre Dumas, in *Le grand dictionnaire de cuisines*, paints a vivid portrait of thirteenth-century Parisian sauce hawkers. They ran through the streets of Paris at dinnertime, he tells us, crying, "Mustard sauce! . . . Garlic sauce! . . . Scallion sauce! . . . Verjuice sauce! . . . *Ravigote* sauce! . . . " Parisians eager for sauces for their meat opened their windows and called their preference to the peddlers. Whether or not there was mustard in Dijon at the time, whether the cries were heard only on the streets of Paris or also along Dijon's rue de la Liberté, we can envision modern mustard in its early years.

In the year 1254, secular vinegar makers were granted permission to make mustard as well as vinegar. By 1292, the Parisian tax register listed ten *moutardiers*. At the same time, the mixture that would eventually become the touchstone for French mustard was being developed in Dijon. There, the first written reference came in 1336 and the first regulations governing its production in 1390. At that time, it was stated simply that the mustard must be soaked in and mixed with good vinegar, as opposed to spoiled wine, as was often the practice. In addition, it was required to age for twelve days before being sold.

The next several decades saw an increase in the regulation of mustard and its makers, the creation of inspectors, and the formation of mustard-maker guilds and corporations. Still, it seems that adulteration and contamination persisted until the middle of the sixteenth century, when regulations were instituted governing the cleanliness of all utensils used in the production of mustard. In 1658, additional laws protected mustard producers, making it an offense for anyone else to make the sauce. A substantial fine and the confiscation of the unauthorized product rendered it unprofitable for others to attempt to compete with the official mustard makers of France.

In spite of the wide acceptance of mustard and the regulations governing its production, it appears that its popularity was on the decline in the early eighteenth century. The House of Maille, founded in 1747, was doing well in Paris, but general interest in the condiment had ebbed, in part because of competition from spices newly available from the Americas and the Far East. The market was revived, and the city of Dijon as the capital of mustard secured, when, in 1856, Burgundian Jean Naigeon substituted verjuice for the vinegar that had been used in nearly all

French mustard preparations. The use of verjuice—the juice of unripe grapes—resulted in a mustard that was less acidic and less pungent than France had tasted before, and thus the smooth, suave condiment assumed its place in history.

By this time, many of the proprietors whose names we recognize on today's mustard labels were setting up shop and the revived interest in mustard allowed room for them all. The House of Maille, which currently offers eight flavored mustards, then had twenty-four varieties, including nasturtium mustard, anchovy mustard, garlic mustard, and mustard with truffles. The enduring house, which today is part of a conglomerate that includes Grey Poupon, supplied mustard to Madame de Pompadour. The House of Bordin, Maille's main competitor, offered forty different mustards, including varieties flavored with rose, with vanilla, and with garlic. In 1777, the company that would become known as Grey Poupon was founded, although Maurice Grey did not arrive on the scene until 1834 and his partner, Auguste Poupon, not until 1866. Grey revolutionized the mustard industry when he invented new machinery that greatly streamlined the production of mustard without sacrificing its quality. With his new automation, production rose from about thirty-five pounds a day per person to over a hundred pounds per day. The company flourished, and when Napoleon III ate mustard, it bore the name Grey Poupon.

Alexandre Bornibus, a Burgundian who established himself as a Parisian mustard maker, became fashionable not only for the taste and variety of his mustards, but for two distinct types, men's mustard and ladies' mustard. It was his claim that a "lady's palate" was more delicate and sensitive than a man's and thus typical Dijon mustard was too strong for women. Accurate or not, this distinction drew a great deal of attention to the new mustard maker. Bornibus was obviously quite adept at marketing, and Alexander Dumas's lengthy essay on mustard, which he claimed was inspired by an anonymous correspondent who forced a public response by not including a return address, was actually an advertisement commissioned by the astute Paris businessman. The article, originally published in 1873, concludes with the author's chance discovery of Bornibus's mustards and his delight upon tasting them. Bornibus's original little shop at 60 boulevard de la Villette survives today and is run by his direct descendants.

Mustard's popularity continued to flourish in the nineteenth century, but the number of mustard makers began a steady decline as large companies absorbed smaller producers. In 1865, there were thirty-nine mustard manufacturers in Dijon; by 1911, their numbers had decreased to ten. All the while, the French government continued to regulate the industry closely, and in 1937, the regulations were strengthened into laws. Only black mustard or brown mustard can be used in French mustards, except in Alsace and Lorraine, where a preparation of white mustard is traditional. Verjuice, wine, and wine vinegar are the permitted liquids, and spices, salt, water, and sulphur dioxide can be added. If the prepared mustard contains any other ingredients—flour, white mustard seed or flour, eggs, oil—it must be labeled as a condiment and not as a mustard. At this same time, Dijon was granted an *appellation contrôlée*, a designation of origin generally granted only to wines. Although the designation requires a specific method rather than a location of production, nearly all Dijon mustard comes from Dijon and the surrounding area.

Other regions of France developed their own styles of mustard, but none succeeded in capturing the favor of the rest of the country, or indeed, of the world, like the mustard of Dijon. Just two styles remain popular today. Pommery is perhaps the brand most familiar to us. This is the whole-grain mustard of Meaux, characterized by its sharp vinegar flavor and crunchy whole mustard seeds. The Pommery family took over the company in 1760, and their mustard is said to have been praised by noted connoisseur Jean Anthelme Brillat-Savarin as the finest in the world. The mustard of Bordeaux, similarly coarse-grained and tart although spicier than that of Meaux, remains a popular condiment today.

The Romans probably introduced mustard to the English as well as to the French, although the history of the spice is harder to trace once it reaches England. Shakespeare mentions a mustard made in Tewkesbury in the six-

24

He a good wit! hang him baboon!
His wit is as thick as Tewkesbury mustard.

> Falstaff, in William Shakespeare's
> *Henry IV*

teenth century, but no records of the once flourishing business survive today. The seeds of Tewskesbury mustard were washed, pounded, and sifted, and the resulting mustard flour was mixed with cold water infused with horseradish. The mustard was shaped into balls that were then dried, making them easy to transport and to store. To prepare the mustard, a piece was broken off and reconstituted with a liquid: buttermilk, vinegar, beer, red wine, cherry juice, or cider. Occasionally other flavorings—spices, honey, sugar— were added. The resulting mustard was very thick and very hot. As popular as Tewkesbury mustard was for a time, it disappeared suddenly, with no written record and no specific recipes left behind.

It wasn't long before another English region spawned a celebrity mustard maker. Mrs. Clements of Durham became enormously popular when she took to grinding mustard seeds and sifting them through fine cloth exactly as if she were milling wheat. Although she was not the first to process mustard in this way, she seems to have been the most industrious. She kept her method and her recipe secret, and built up a very successful mustard trade until she sold her business to King George I.

Although other mustard companies flourished in England, most notably Keen & Sons, founded in 1747, the next English mustard producer to make an enduring name for

himself would not come along until 1804. In that year, Jeremiah Colman, a miller of flour, began the first of several expansions that would make his name a synonym for mustard. Today, we recognize the bright yellow tins of ground mustard that sit on nearly every market shelf in the country. Colman's is a name synonymous with English mustard, just as Dijon is synonymous with French mustard.

Colman's technique was similar to that of Mrs. Clements and the crucial element was that the mustard seed was ground without heating it, so that there was no subsequent release of oil that heating would cause. Today, Colman's mustard is prepared by much the same process that Jeremiah Colman developed. Two types of mustard seed, white and brown, are ground separately and sifted through silk cloth to separate the husks and the bran from the mustard flour. Originally, black mustard seed was used, but it was replaced by brown several decades ago. After grinding and sifting, the two types of mustard are mixed together and packaged in the famous yellow tins. This blend of the two types of mustard provides a full range of sensation on the tongue, along with the pungent, vaporizing effects created only by the brown mustard.

Colman's greatest contribution, and the reason for his company's rapid expansion, was not necessarily mustard itself, although it did and does turn out a consistent high-quality product. More importantly, Colman was brilliant at promoting his mustard. The company's packaging is striking: the name *Colman's* appears in red letters on a bright yellow background, with the signature bull's head alongside. The image is bold and memorable. In addition to striking graphics, effective advertising campaigns captured the public's attention. The most dramatic campaign was the creation of the Mustard Club (see sidebar). The company produced special mustard tins each Christmas for over fifty years, along with illustrated children's books that were given away during the holiday season. Although Colman's made its name with its mustard flour, still its most popular product, it introduced other preparations beginning in 1933. In that year, Colman's created the first food product sold in a tube, a prepared mustard. Today, the company makes several types of prepared mustards, including a Dijon-style preparation, but none compete in either quality or popularity with Colman's dry mustard.

One of the more surprising aspects of contemporary

commercial mustard production is the amount of secrecy that surrounds the industry. Although the variables in mustard production are limited, mustard makers guard their individual secrets like precious gems kept hidden far from the light of day. A visit to a large mustard-processing plant in all likelihood reveals no privileged information at all, yet it is virtually impossible to gain access. All mustard is made in relatively the same way. The seed must be crushed, its hull and bran sifted out or not depending on the type of mustard being made. It then may or may not go through further grinding and crushing. A liquid such as water, wine, vinegar, beer, or a combination of several of these liquids must be added, along with seasonings and perhaps other flavorings. The mustard must be mixed and in some cases simmered and then cooled. Some mustard is aged in large containers before it is bottled, but eventually all of it is put into some sort of container to be shipped to its customer.

None of the subtle details—the specific spices or their amounts, the type of liquid, the quantity of salt or the lack thereof—can be detected from observing the process, yet one is almost always refused access. The recipe for Grey Poupon, now owned domestically by R. J. R. Nabisco, Inc., is kept in a locked safe at all times, and it is said that no one ever speaks about it. That Grey Poupon is now made in California in addition to France—a fact that many would consider an asset—is closely guarded, played down, not advertised. Smaller producers, those that make mustards for a variety of labels, for example, are more generous about whom they allow to observe the mixing and the blending, the boiling and the bottling.

There is something about mustard that seems to inspire zaniness, a sort of goofy pursuit of a mustard obsession, a phenomenon I had encountered previously only with garlic. This silliness is not a recent development, however. The Mustard Club and its adjunct, the Order of the Bath, stand out as the most dramatic and sophisticated examples of the humor that so often surrounds the condiment.

In May 1922, noted British author Dorothy L. Sayers accepted a position as copywriter with one of London's largest advertising agencies, Benson's. Among the projects she worked on was a large campaign commissioned by Colman's. The Mustard Club was the focus of the agency's efforts. The club was full of Sayers's signature talent not only for pun, parody, and rampant good humor, but also for intelligence and historical resonance. The far-reaching campaign included a mock lawsuit against a restaurant for not making its mustard fresh daily and a prospectus of the Mustard Club credited Aesculapius, the god of medicine, with being its original founder. The club's officers in particular bear the mark of the creator of everybody's favorite detective, the charming Lord Peter Wimsey. Among the fictional participants were Master Mustard; Lord Bacon of Cookham; the Baron de Beef, president of the club; and Miss Di Gester, its secretary. A short film produced at the time immortalizes the characters during the trial of a man accused of attempting to eat a ham sandwich without mustard. The crucial evidence is given by the sandwich itself; the offender is found guilty and condemned to soak in a mustard bath, to which he is promptly escorted.

The club published the Recipe Book of the Mustard Club, *also penned by Dorothy Sayers, who was herself an accomplished cook. Although the club began as a marketing gimmick and without membership solicitation, hundreds of mustard enthusiasts wrote to request membership and were accommodated. A card game was developed, as were several club songs and a monthly newsletter. The Mustard Club became quite fashionable and was the feature of many news items and cartoons of its time. The campaign was considered one of Benson's great successes, and it certainly did the trick, focusing attention and glamour on a humble condiment. The club lasted for seven years, and vanished during the difficult years of the Depression.*

The spirit of the Mustard Club has been revived today by Barry Levenson and a score of other mustard producers whose recipe brochures often reveal as much about their humor as they do about mustard itself.

MUSTARD IN THE KITCHEN

Mustard in the kitchen has three primary functions: as a condiment, as a flavoring agent or spice, and as a vegetable when one includes pickled mustard root, mustard greens, mustard sprouts, and certain other members of the large *Cruciferae* family. Although both dry and prepared mustards serve as condiments and flavoring agents, they have vastly different characteristics. It is important to understand and use them correctly. Mustard also has good emulsifying ability. It can help bind a sauce, and is used commercially to create the proper texture in sausages and prepared meat products.

As condiments, prepared commercial or homemade mustards are used just as they are, out of the jar or bottle to enhance sandwiches and other prepared foods. A simple piece of grilled fish is enlivened by a spoonful of your favorite mustard, and certain foods—roast beef in England, for example, and sausages in Germany—are rarely served without a spoonful or more of mustard on the side. It takes no particular skill or knowledge to use mustard in this way, simply access to a good selection of condiments and a lively palate that appreciates mustard's good flavor.

The use of mustard flour as a condiment is most common in Asian cuisine, where the flour made from brown seeds is mixed with water or rice vinegar to form the hot spicy sauce we all recognize when we order, say, egg rolls. Mustard in this form is hot and sharp, without the nuance and subtlety of more suave European preparations. It serves its purpose in the same way that *wasabi*, the Japanese horseradish served with sushi and sashimi, offers a bright flash, a counterpoint to the richness of raw fish, or the way mustard complements the rich textures and flavors of an egg roll, both palate cleansers with a strong punch. Again, it takes no special skill and little knowledge to prepare mustard in this way. The one thing to remember is that the liquid—water or vinegar—should be as cold as possible. Mustard flour mixed with a warm or hot liquid will be bitter.

Mustard as a flavoring agent requires a little more knowledge to use skillfully. To use prepared mustard in this way, be sure to begin with a product whose flavor you like. Although there are scores, several hundred actually, of pre-

COMMERCIAL MUSTARDS

TYPE	CHARACTERISTICS	RECOMMENDED STORAGE	USES
Flour, mild (one of the standard retail dry mustards)	Pale yellow powder, heat on tongue	Pantry, well sealed against dampness	Mild homemade mustard; as a spice; pickling
Flour, hot (one of the standard retail dry mustards)	Deep yellow powder, full vaporizing heat	Pantry, well sealed against dampness	Chinese-style mustard; homemade mustards; as a spice in sauces, dressings; pickling
Colman's Dry	Mix of mild and hot mustard flours	Pantry, well sealed against dampness	English hot mustard; Chinese-style mustard; homemade mustards; as a spice in sauces, dressings; pickling
Seeds, white	Pale yellow seeds	Pantry, well sealed against dampness	Homemade coarse-grain mustard; pickling; Indian spice blends; garnish; sprouts
Seeds, brown	Tiny reddish black seeds	Pantry, well sealed against dampness	Homemade Dijon-style mustard; Indian spice blends; sprouts
American yellow	Sharply acidic but without much heat; made from white mustard seeds only	Refrigeration is not essential, but will help maintain maximum flavor	The basic hot-dog mustard

TYPE	CHARAC-TERISTICS	RECOMMENDED STORAGE	USES
American brown	Mild with a bit of spiciness, less acidic than American yellow	Refrigeration is not essential, but will help maintain maximum flavor	As a condiment if you prefer a very mild mustard
English hot	Full taste on the tongue and full vaporization; very hot	Refrigeration is not essential, but will help maintain maximum flavor	As a condiment with smoked meats, Cheddar cheese, sausages, roast beef
Dijon	Typical Dijon that has been toned down some	Refrigeration is not essential, but will help maintain maximum flavor	As a condiment; in marinades, sauces, dressings
Dijon, extra strong, for export	Smooth, suave French mustard, more pungent than Dijon, but less so than that produced for domestic use (in France)	Refrigeration is not essential, but will help maintain maximum flavor	As a condiment; in marinades, sauces, dressings
Dijon, extra-forte, French	Smooth, suave French mustard with full range of pungency	Refrigeration is not essential, but will help maintain maximum flavor	As a condiment; in marinades, sauces, dressings
Bordeaux	Made with whole brown seeds, sweet, spicy, tart	Pantry	As a condiment, on sandwiches, with smoked meats and pâtés

TYPE	CHARAC-TERISTICS	RECOMMENDED STORAGE	USES
Meaux	Made with whole brown seeds, slightly spicy, very tart, not sweet	Pantry	As a condiment, on sandwiches, with smoked meats and pâtés
German hot	Brown, often hot, frequently sweet, and often flavored with horseradish	Refrigeration is not essential, but will help maintain maximum flavor	As a condiment with sausages, smoked meats, pâtés
Creole	Vary with producer, most often slightly coarse-grain brown mustard, rather tart	Refrigeration may not be essential, but will help maintain flavor; check ingredients list	As a condiment
Dijon style	Many have an unpleasant floury texture; generally inferior in all ways to French mustards	Refrigeration is not essential, but will help maintain maximum flavor	Limited, unless you find one you particularly like
Flavored Dijon style	Quality and characteristics vary greatly, as do flavors; those made with true Dijon tend to be best	Refrigeration often essential; check ingredients list	As a condiment
Other flavored mustards	Quality and characteristics vary greatly	Refrigeration often essential; check ingredients list	As a condiment

pared mustards and mustard condiments available in the retail marketplace, just a few should be considered for use in this way. Certainly, choose whatever you like as a condiment, but it is not necessary to use flavored and generally expensive specialty mustards in most cooking. I keep three or four Dijon mustards and two or three coarse-grain mustards in my pantry for general cooking purposes (see The Annotated Mustard Pantry, page 43), usually adding other ingredients such as honey, green peppercorns, jalapeños, lemon juice, herbs, and spices separately. Not only is this a less expensive way to cook, but it also, I believe, produces the best results because you control both the amount of each ingredient and its freshness. If you want your final dish to taste of tarragon, for example, add fresh or dried tarragon rather than use a tarragon mustard. The flavors will be brighter, fresher, and cleaner.

To maintain maximum flavor, mustard should be added later rather than earlier in the cooking process, as heat destroys much of mustard's distinctive taste. Mustard should also be added with a keen awareness of the balance of flavors. A delicate *beurre blanc* is delightful with a small amount of Dijon-style mustard added—a teaspoon, perhaps—but more would overwhelm the lightness of the sauce. On the other hand, a teaspoon of prepared mustard would barely be noticed in a heartier mixture like a marinade and substantially more would need to be added.

Mustard flour is part of many a spice cabinet, where it is used in Indian spice mixtures, pickling spice (both the seed and mustard flour), and as part of countless traditional recipes such as gingerbread and chocolate cake. It contributes a richness and a depth of flavor that is not necessarily identified as mustard, but is essential nonetheless. There are many claims that mustard flour heightens the flavors of all foods, much as monosodium glutamate does. Although the statement never has been scientifically verified, it is often the case that mustard appears in unlikely recipes and perhaps this is why. Generally, mustard flour is used as you use other spices and requires no special treatment.

In salad dressings and other emulsified sauces, mustard contributes not only its flavor and its heat, but also its ability to hold an oil and water mixture in suspension. It can help keep a hollandaise sauce or a homemade mayonnaise from separating, and a vinaigrette with a substantial amount of mustard—either dry or prepared—will stay blended longer than a sauce without it.

MUSTARD AND HEALTH

Like most foods with ancient roots, mustard has been heralded as a curative with a variety of healing properties. It also has been reviled, however briefly, as a poison and its advocates dismissed as lunatics. The source of these latter claims are harder to substantiate than the claims of mustard's healing effects, many of which can be readily documented today.

Mustard stimulates appetite and digestion, and it clears the sinuses in much the same way as chilies, which are said to be as effective as nearly all commercial decongestants. It is a preservative and inhibits the growth of a variety of yeasts, molds, and bacteria. It increases blood circulation, hence its use as mustard plaster, a dressing used to bring increased blood flow to inflamed areas of the body. In the past, it has been used to treat asthma, bronchitis, pleurisy, and pneumonia. Although mustard has generally been taken orally or applied directly to the skin in the form of a mustard plaster, mustard baths are said to be curative, too. Mustard's stimulating effects work in this medium, although the one commercially available mustard bath, Dr. Singha's, is so full of the scents of wintergreen and eucalyptus that it smells like a sickroom. Even so, it is an unbeatable remedy for chilled feet on a winter day. Mustard flour sprinkled in your socks is said to save your toes from frostbite, a claim that is also made about cayenne pepper and other spices containing volatile oils. Indeed, there are mixtures of mustard, ginger, and cayenne pepper that are sold to winter hikers and skiers as footwarming preparations. They do work if conditions are not overly severe.

Native Americans in the western United States had particularly interesting uses for the herb they found growing wild in the Rocky Mountain regions. They used mustard to fight cold symptoms and headaches, to counter sciatic pain, to bring on menstruation, to ease the difficulty of childbirth, and to subdue the causes and discomfort of swollen testicles. Native Americans were aware also of mustard's effectiveness as an emetic, and learned to rinse wild mustard cabbage in several water baths before eating it.

Mustard was once an ingredient in smelling salts, and in ancient times mustard seeds were chewed to relieve the symptoms of toothache. Today, those remedies that take advantage of mustard's stimulating qualities—of the blood and of the appetite—remain relevant, although they are used less than they once were.

One of mustard's greatest health benefits is that it provides tremendous flavor for few calories and little fat. A gram of mustard flour contains just 4.3 calories, and simple mustard preparations can be eaten with impunity by nearly everyone. Mustard itself contains no cholesterol, has only trace amounts of vegetable fat, and is between 25 and 32 percent protein, depending on the variety of plant. Leaf mustard is particularly rich in vitamins A and C and in calcium (about as much as milk), and also contains considerable vitamin B, phosphorus, and magnesium.

For each taster provide:
A small bowl full of thin pretzel sticks
A large glass of unflavored sparkling water
An evaluation sheet (see Tasting Notes, page 208) and a
  pencil
A napkin

On the common table place:
Up to one dozen different mustards
Ramekins or custard cups filled with 3 or 4 table-
  spoons of the mustards to be tasted, placed in front of
  their corresponding jars of mustard
Bottles or pitchers of chilled sparkling water
Additional pretzel sticks

MUSTARD TASTING

Organized tastings of foods and food products have grown in popularity for the last number of years. A gourmet shop offers samples of several different raspberry vinegars; friends gather together to taste a half-dozen boutique olive oils; farmers' markets hold special tastings of summer's fruits and vegetables. It is a very good marketing tool, a way to introduce customers to new items and to educate them as to what they like and don't like and why. A good tasting is one where you learn something, not just chow down on free goodies.

Such a tasting is also an excellent way for friends to navigate the multitude of new food products appearing on shelves throughout the country. Faced with scores of new olive oils—many of them very expensive—dozens of unfamiliar vinegars, hundreds of mustards, how is the consumer to make intelligent choices without depleting the food budget? I always suggest that a group of food lovers get together, coordinate their choices so that no brand is duplicated, and organize a tasting. It keeps expenses to a minimum while offering the opportunity to taste a whole pantryful of new products. With mustards, it is an inexpensive, interesting, and delicious occasion, even somewhat refreshing and invigorating. Whereas olive oil and vinegar tastings often leave the palate exhausted and the tasters informed but rather overwhelmed, a mustard tasting can conclude with a hearty feast if everyone is so inclined. Mustard is an appetite stimulant, and we can consume a fair amount of the pungent sauce before we tire.

To taste mustards, gather together all of the ingredients listed in the tasting menu. The pretzel sticks serve as "spoons" for sampling the mustard. Take a little of one mustard on a pretzel stick and then taste the mustard from the pretzel. Don't eat the pretzel at the same time because its texture and flavor will interfere with your experience of the mustard. Discard the pretzel after each taste of mustard. It is helpful to refresh your palate with sparkling water after every couple of tastes. Continue the tasting until everyone has become familiar with all of the mustards and made appropriate notes.

What do we look for when tasting mustard? Although taste is largely subjective, there are certain objective criteria to consider when evaluating the condiment. First of all, the mustard should be entirely pleasant. It should be somewhat acidic, but not overly so, and it should not be too salty. Its flavors should be well balanced, with no single element dominating. If it is sweet, for example, sugar should not be the predominant taste, merely an element of the whole. The texture should be smooth or, in the case of coarse-grain mustard, pleasantly grainy, not gritty or hard. It should have a fairly thick consistency, so that it easily holds its own shape on a spoon, but it should not be so thick as to be cloying or tongue-coating. Mustard should not taste floury, musty, or metallic; nor should it taste or smell eggy. Even if it is hot, it should not burn the tongue. Mustard always should have a pleasant aftertaste, a harmonious finish on the palate as the flavors fade together. If it vaporizes so that your eyes water and forehead sweats but you are eager for more, consider yourself lucky and be sure to write down the name of that mustard.

When tasting for comparison, taste mustards of a similar type, all Dijon, for example, or all sweet-hot. Judge Dijon mustards for their smooth texture, the balance of acid, the depth of flavor. If tasting to discover new mustards, simply choose ones you have been wanting to try or those that seem interesting. Mustards, unlike, say, vinegars or wines, will not compete with or overwhelm each other.

PART TWO

The Annotated Mustard Pantry

IT IS EASY FOR EITHER THE ENTHUSIASTIC OR THE reluctant home cook to keep a helpful supply of good mustards in the pantry, and there are several important reasons to do so. First, if you want to incorporate a variety of mustards into your cooking, you should have them at hand, rather than having to run to the market when a recipe calls for them. The mustards I recommend here should allow you to complete nearly any recipe requiring mustard. Second, a comprehensive supply of mustards will help you grow as a cook. With them at your fingertips, there on your shelf each time you open the pantry, they will inspire you. You will become adept at using them, and that use will start to bear your signature. Finally, mustards are great in an emergency.

If friends show up unexpectedly, if you can't get to the market for a few days, a good supply of mustards will assist you in almost any culinary emergencies that arise.

MUSTARD LABELS

In general, it is a good idea to get into the habit of reading the labels of the foods we buy, particularly the ingredients portion. Names of products can be deceptive, especially with something like mustard, which has no legal definition, unlike, say, vinegar. If a product is labeled simply "vinegar," United States law requires that it be apple cider vinegar and nothing else. A product labeled as mustard has no such legal requirement or guarantee. In addition to mustard, it can include vinegar, wine, beer, oil, eggs, flour, and any number of spices, additives, or preservatives. Indeed, a product labeled as mustard is not required to contain mustard. I came across such a condiment and when I queried its maker, the response was that the mustard was included in the ingredient listing of "spices." Fortunately, however, there is, in most instances, a larger portion of mustard in products sold as mustard, mustard sauce, or mustard condiment.

Prepared mustard is a simple mixture and should contain only whole mustard seeds, mustard flour, liquid, spices, salt, pepper, and sometimes sugar. It would be helpful if labeling guidelines required that preparations with ingredients other than these be labeled as condiments, but since there is no such requirement, we must be watchful. Additional ingredients influence not only the taste of the product, but the amount of calories, the percentage of those calories that are fat, and the way in which the condiment must be stored.

Flavored mustards in particular may contain any number of ingredients other than those required to make a simple mustard paste. These additional ingredients—eggs, fruits, vegetables, and juices, for example—are often perishable, and condiments containing them should be stored in the refrigerator rather than on the pantry shelf. Although true mustards can be stored in the pantry, it is dangerous to leave *all* mustard condiments on the shelf without verifying their stability first. Over time, mustard loses its pungency; refrigeration will slow the loss of flavor.

It is fashionable these days for a variety of businesses, particularly wineries and specialty stores, to feature their own mustards, although few of these mustards are actually made by the facilities that sell them. Rather, they are produced by large wholesalers who offer specialty labeling. Buy these products when you like them, but remember that they are often more expensive than similar products found in general markets, and don't be fooled into thinking you're choosing a handcrafted product. Only rarely are these condiments made from recipes unique to the businesses whose labels they display.

These are the pantry mustards I consider essential.

Dijon:

Three jars of a good Dijon for cooking purposes, with two jars on the pantry shelf for daily usage and one jar in the refrigerator for culinary emergencies (like having forgotten to restock your pantry); one jar of Dijon extra-forte; one or more of the best (i.e., your favorite) Dijon for use as a condiment.

Coarse-grain mustard:

Three types, with one smooth and balanced, one tart, and one sweet.

Flavored:

Those flavored mustards you like in amounts that will be used within four to six months. I keep several mustards flavored with sweet onions, one commercial honey mustard, one green peppercorn mustard, and one Dijon with lemon.

Mustard flour:

Mild; hot; and Colman's.

Seeds:

Yellow and brown.

Other Mustard Products:

Mustard oil and pickled mustard root (optional, except for cooks who love Asian cuisines).

SHOPPING FOR MUSTARD PRODUCTS *Certain mustard products are difficult to come by in your neighborhood supermarket. Although you will find mustard flour, and possibly mustard seeds, in the spice section, they will be in small containers, and therefore impractical for use in recipes that may call for as much as a cup or more. A wholesale food distributor that sells directly to the public is your best bet for purchasing mustard seeds and mustard flour in bulk. Natural foods stores often carry these items in bulk as well.*

A GLOSSARY OF COMMERCIAL MUSTARDS

AMERICAN BROWN MUSTARD The classic delicatessen mustard, this mixture is brown, less tart than ballpark mustard, and mildly spicy but not hot. It is traditionally used in red-eye gravy.

AMERICAN MUSTARD This mustard accounts for 75 percent of all mustard eaten in the United States. It is made from ground white mustard seeds, turmeric, and vinegar, and has a bright, sharp taste. It certainly belongs on hot dogs, but has limited culinary uses.

BALLPARK MUSTARD Same as American Mustard.

BLACK MUSTARD Generally indicates an English prepared mustard made with whole brown seeds, molasses, and sometimes beer.

47

CHINESE MUSTARD A simple mixture of hot mustard flour and water, with little nuance but lots of fire.

COARSE-GRAIN MUSTARD Mustard made, at least in part, with whole mustard seeds; England, Germany, and France all produce distinctive versions. The French types tend to be sharply acidic, while the English and the German are often sweet.

CREOLE MUSTARD Although many products may bear this designation, it is generally a simple preparation of coarse-ground seeds, vinegar, and possibly horseradish and sugar.

DIJON A smooth, elegant mustard with an extremely fine texture, a strong but not overbearing acidic element, and a subtle play of herbs and spices; some Dijon mustards can be quite pungent, although those made for export are milder than those made for French consumption.

DIJON, EXTRA-FORTE The same mustard as Dijon, but with its full force of vaporizing pungency.

DIJON STYLE Dijon is a protected name, and must be made according to specific guidelines set in 1937 by the French government. Grey Poupon is the only true Dijon mustard made outside of France. Other mustards that attempt to duplicate Dijon's characteristics must be labeled "Dijon style"; some work, most don't.

MUSTARD FLOUR, HOT The powdered endosperm of brown mustard, it has mustard's full potency. Mustard flour is commonly found in the spice sections of retail markets and labeled as mustard, dry mustard, ground mustard, or mustard powder.

MUSTARD FLOUR, MILD The powdered endosperm of white mustard. Its heat is felt only on the tongue, and it is often quite bitter if mixed directly with an acid or if it is not allowed sufficient aging. Labeled as mustard, dry mustard, or ground mustard, it is usually found in the spice sections of retail markets.

ENGLISH MUSTARD Generally made with a blend of hot and mild mustard flours and with whole seeds, this mustard can be either dry or prepared. Colman's (dry), a blend of white and brown mustard flours, is the best known of the classic English mustards.

FLAVORED MUSTARD A mustard condiment that, rather than being made in a particular style (Dijon or Creole, for example), is flavored with any number of herbs, spices, aromatics, vegetables, fruits, or juices.

GERMAN MUSTARD May be coarse-grain or smooth, but most German mustards are hot and often sweet, and brown rather than yellow.

JAPANESE MUSTARD Generally refers to a purplish green leafy vegetable that is either a component of salad mixes (when harvested small) or sold separately (when harvested more mature).

MUSTARD OIL Generally indicates pure mustard oil extracted from the seed of *Brassica juncea*. Recently a product named mustard oil appeared on the market that is a blend of mustard oil and canola oil flavored with mustard flour. It is quite good.

Mustard seed, brown Available commercially in the spice section of many supermarkets, this is the seed of *Brassica juncea*.

Mustard seed, white This is generally what you get when you buy a product labeled simply as mustard seed. It is the seed of *Brassica alba*, and the one most commonly used in pickling spice.

Mustard-flavored oil Any oil that has been flavored with mustard seeds or mustard flour.

Oriental mustard In the commercial mustard industry, oriental mustard refers to yellow *Brassica juncea* (brown mustard). In common usage, the term refers to a simple paste of water and hot mustard flour.

Pickled mustard root The roots of *Brassica juncea* pickled and used in pork balls and other Chinese dishes.

Russian mustard Generally refers to a sweet mustard made with brown or oriental mustard so that it has its full range of flavor.

Sweet-hot mustard There are numerous mustards labeled as sweet-hot and they vary a great deal. Sometimes these mustards are called California-style, named, perhaps, for the number of boutique mustard producers in the state.

PART THREE

A Mustard
Cookbook

51

COOKING WITH MUSTARD

There are thousands of recipes that call for mustard, from simple mixtures of commercial mayonnaise and ballpark mustard combined quickly as a sauce for grilled fish (I had this once, with salmon that had been swimming just a few hours before; it was great) to complex soups, sauces, stews, breads, and pickles that use one or more of mustard's many culinary properties to enliven them. Because of the great diversity of mustards and their uses, this was a difficult book to write. What do I want the recipes to offer the reader? I asked myself over and over, as I added new recipes and discarded old ones, as I revived some and sent others to the alternate file for a second and third time. I wanted, when I first conceived of this book, to present mustard recipes in a historical context, showing how the use of the ubiquitous plant in all its forms—herb, spice, condiment, vegetable—has changed over the centuries, how it has remained the same, the ways in which it continues to inspire cooks from diverse cultures with its pungency and power. There is a historical record that needs to be preserved, I told myself, and classical traditions and recipes that need to be honored.

When I struggled one terribly stormy weekend preparing time-honored recipes such as tongue in mustard-vinegar sauce, rabbit stew in a mustard marinade, and chicken livers with coarse-grain mustard, the book began to take its present form. I had lamb's kidneys, plump and perfectly rare, and sweetbreads in a fragrant mustard reduction sauce, and no one at all eager to try either one of them. They were all wonderfully rich and delicious, full of good flavors that evoked an earlier time and, alas, an older style of eating and of thinking. Here in the United States in the health-conscious 1990s, we eat less red meat and fewer innards, or organ meats, than our parents or their parents before them. Certainly, we find all of these foods offered in good restaurants and delicatessens, and some of us treat ourselves occasionally, but, in general, we cook foods that are considered healthier and more environmentally friendly.

The Good Cook's Book of Mustard was, I realized then, a contemporary cookbook, a collection of good recipes that people will use today. A historical subtext informs the narrative, offering perspective, context, and anecdote to increase our knowledge of one of the world's most popular seasonings. But the recipes themselves stand on their own and feature easy-to-find ingredients, a contemporary style, an ease of preparation, and an eye toward considerations of health. There are a few exceptions, such as my favorite recipe for beef tongue with mustard. And no book on mustards should omit mustard's venerable marriage with beef, but here America's most popular meat appears primarily in smaller portions than, say, the once popular sixteen-ounce steak or the centerpiece of roast beef or prime rib. The flavor and texture of beef and the way it is enhanced by mustard are featured in recipes that take advantage of its good qualities while limiting its quantity. I do not believe these good foods should be entirely abandoned, but rather fit into our diet with an eye towards balance, health, diversity, and ecology.

Finally, I want to add a word about my philosophy of cooking and of the function of recipes. The requirements of writing often make a recipe seem cast in stone, as if each specific measurement and technique were of more importance than is often the case. In many instances, there is something arbitrary about the choices a chef makes when committing to paper a particular combination of ingredients or way of blending them. I believe there is more than one way to produce a desired result, and we see this over and over as each cook leaves his or her own signature on every dish. Thus, when I list, say, chutney in a recipe and give no further instructions, do not wonder which chutney I want you to use. Rather, choose a chutney you prefer or discover a new one. Work from the spirit of a recipe, but develop the

A NOTE ABOUT SALT All the recipes in this book were tested using kosher salt, a coarse-grain salt without additives. I use this salt because I prefer both its taste and texture over regular fine-grain table salt. Because kosher salt is flakier and less dense than standard commercial salt, some adjustment in quantity may be necessary. A recipe that calls for one teaspoon of kosher salt may require only half or three quarters that amount of fine-grain salt. Regarding salt in general, I do not recommend omitting it entirely unless you have a specific medical condition that is made worse with the intake of salt. Although the use of salt is currently out of favor, only an extremely small segment of the population is adversely affected by its consumption. Salt is an essential seasoning that heightens the taste of nearly all foods; savory foods do not reach their full flavor without its skillful application. Salt draws the disparate elements of a dish together and, because it melts slowly on the tongue, contributes to the harmonious blending of flavors and creates a pleasant finish on the palate.

skill and, most of all, the confidence, to adapt it to your own style and preferences.

LITTLE RECIPES

Mustard Dipping Sauce Mix together ¼ cup of your favorite flavored mustard with ½ cup All-Purpose Mustard Sauce (page 188). The sauce will be full of mustard's vaporizing heat as well as the flavors of the particular mustard you choose. Serve as a dip for crudités, pretzels, or sliced sausages.

Artichokes with Mustard Mayonnaise Mix together 2 tablespoons homemade or high-quality prepared mayonnaise and 2 teaspoons extra-strong Dijon mustard or any favorite flavored mustard. Serve as a dip with hot or chilled artichokes.

Asparagus Cook asparagus spears until just tender and fan out on a platter; place a bowl of Honey-Ginger Mustard (page 175) in the center of the platter. If available, garnish with pesticide-free mustard flowers. Serve hot or chilled. This makes a great appetizer, especially in late winter when the first asparagus is available.

Asparagus with Prosciutto For 4 people, steam or boil 16 stalks of trimmed asparagus until just tender. Refresh in cold water and drain. Brush 16 paper-thin slices of imported prosciutto with Dijon mustard and wrap each stalk of asparagus in one of the slices, leaving about 3 inches of the asparagus tip exposed. Serve immediately as an appetizer or as part of an antipasto platter.

Baked Potatoes with Mustard Butter Serve baked potatoes with Mustard Butter (page 185) and with sour cream mixed with Dijon mustard.

Tomatoes Vinaigrette Arrange thick slices of ripe in-season tomatoes on a plate and top with your favorite mustard vinaigrette (suggestions on page 183–184).

Baked Tomatoes Cut about ½ inch off the stem ends of several ripe in-season tomatoes. Spread the surface of each tomato with Dijon mustard—plain or flavored with green peppercorns, basil, tarragon, or chives—and top each one with about 1 tablespoon Mustard Bread Crumbs (page 193). Drizzle each one with 1 teaspoon olive oil and bake in a 325°F oven until soft, 15 to 20 minutes.

Leeks in Mustard Vinaigrette Wash carefully and trim a dozen or so young leeks, retaining 2 to 3 inches of the green portion. Plunge into boiling water and simmer until just tender. Drain and hold in ice water. When ready to serve, drain the leeks well, pat dry, and drizzle with Mustard Vinaigrette (page 183). This is a great way to serve the slender French green beans called *haricots verts* as well.

Crudités Accompany a platter of raw and lightly cooked seasonal vegetables with a selection of mustards and mustard sauces. When you choose your condiments, vary the intensity of the mustard so that they complement each other rather than compete. The Mustard Cream on page 186 is mild and subtle, and excellent paired with a more intensely flavored mustard, such as Honey-Ginger Mustard (page 175), Cilantro-Mint Mustard (page 178), or Olive-Anchovy Mustard (page 180). I like to include Mustard Vinaigrette (page 183) and another type of Mustard Cream (page 186) as well.

Macaroni Salad For old-fashioned macaroni salad—loved in the 1950s long before pasta salad became popular—mix 3 parts mayonnaise with 1 part ballpark mustard and toss with salad macaroni, diced celery, and diced onion.

Omelets Mix 1 teaspoon Dijon mustard into every 2 eggs.

Split Pea Soup Use a swirl of Mustard Cream (page 186) on top of each serving of split pea soup.

Broiled Fish Combine your favorite mustard with a little olive oil, brush it on any fish fillet, and broil or bake. Serve with more of the same mustard on the side.

Summer Sandwiches Add a bright spark of heat to summer sandwiches by drizzling them with a tablespoon of mustard oil. Try it with tomatoes, red onion and garlic mayonnaise, or with sweet onions, radishes, thinly sliced potatoes, and shredded purple cabbage.

Grilled Chicken Sandwich Grill a boneless chicken breast or thigh and serve it on a french roll or grilled country bread drizzled with your favorite mustard vinaigrette and a handful of mustard sprouts or whatever greens you prefer.

Grilled Chicken on Walnut Bread Grill a boneless chicken breast. While it is grilling, mix together a little honey and coarse-grain mustard and spread it on your favorite walnut bread. Top with the grilled chicken breast.

Burgers To add a bit of zestiness and richness to your favorite burger—lamb, turkey, or beef—press a coin of Mustard Butter (page 185) into the center before grilling or broiling. My favorite combinations include rosemary-Dijon butter with lamb, sage-Dijon with turkey, and cilantro-mustard butter with beef, into which I've mixed garlic and chopped fresh jalapeño peppers.

Olives in Mustard Seed and Anchovy Marinade

Makes about 4 cups

A big bowl of olives is a beautiful sight. These olives are fragrant and delicious, evocative of the Mediterranean and full of the heat of mustard and garlic. I use a mixture of Kalamata, Niçoise, and Picholine olives for marinating, but any combination you choose is fine. Serve them as an appetizer with hot bread and red wine, or alongside a platter of summer tomatoes. They will keep, refrigerated, for several weeks.

4 cups mixed olives of choice, all with pits or all without

2 tablespoons white mustard seeds

2 tablespoons finely chopped olives

2 tablespoons prepared coarse-grain mustard

1 tablespoon Dijon mustard

5 anchovy fillets, finely minced

2 shallots, finely minced

8 cloves garlic, finely minced

$\frac{1}{4}$ cup balsamic vinegar

$\frac{1}{4}$ cup sherry vinegar

2 teaspoons kosher salt

2 teaspoons freshly ground black pepper

2 teaspoons dried oregano

$\frac{1}{2}$ cup extra virgin olive oil

$1\frac{1}{4}$ cups pure olive oil

Place the whole olives in a large jar or crock. Mix together the mustard seeds, chopped olives, mustards, anchovies, shallots, garlic, vinegars, salt, pepper, and oregano. Whisk in both olive oils, taste the dressing, and adjust the seasonings. Pour over the olives, cover, and let marinate, refrigerated, for at least 24 hours.

Warm to room temperature before serving. The olives will keep for several weeks in the refrigerator.

Marinated Mushrooms with Mustard Seeds

Serves 4 to 6

I enjoy these mushrooms with their bright taste of citrus as part of an antipasto platter. They are particularly good with Asparagus with Prosciutto (page 55) and Tomatoes Vinaigrette (page 56).

1 pound commercial white or Crimini mushrooms
1 cup extra virgin olive oil
$\frac{1}{3}$ cup fresh lemon juice
3 tablespoons extra-forte Dijon mustard
2 tablespoons white mustard seeds

6 cloves of garlic, crushed
Several sprigs of fresh thyme
1 teaspoon black peppercorns
2 teaspoons kosher salt

Clean the mushrooms and trim the stems to remove any dark spots. Place the mushrooms in a nonreactive saucepan. Stir together the olive oil, lemon juice, mustard, mustard seeds, garlic, thyme, peppercorns, and salt and pour the mixture over the mushrooms. Place the pan over medium heat, bring the liquid to a boil, lower the heat, and simmer the mushrooms for 15 minutes, stirring occasionally to ensure that they all are evenly cooked. Remove them from the heat, cool to room temperature, and then refrigerate. The mushrooms should be served slightly chilled or at room temperature, so be sure to remove them about 30 minutes in advance. Serve them in a bowl with small forks or toothpicks. They will keep in the refrigerator for 4 or 5 days.

Carrot Fritters with Mustard Seeds & Mustard Sauce

Makes about 4 dozen 1½-inch fritters

Crunchy, sweet, and savory, these scrumptious fritters spice up any occasion and, served with a ginger-flavored mustard for dipping, make an enticing before-dinner appetizer.

3 cups grated, peeled
  carrots
3 tablespoons minced
  cilantro leaves
1 teaspoon grated fresh
  ginger
1 teaspoon ground cumin
1 tablespoon white mus-
  tard seeds
3 eggs, lightly beaten
3 tablespoons all-purpose
  flour

1½ teaspoons baking
  powder
1 teaspoon kosher salt
1 teaspoon freshly ground
  black pepper
Pure olive oil, peanut oil,
  or canola oil for deep-
  frying
Honey-Ginger Mustard
  Sauce (page 175) or
  Mustard Cream (page
  186)

Mix together all the ingredients except the oil until just combined; be careful not to overmix.

In a deep skillet, pour in oil to a depth of 1½ inches and heat to 350°F. When the oil is ready, drop in the batter, a spoonful at a time, to form each fritter. Be sure not to crowd the pan and allow a few seconds between each fritter to allow the oil to return to the proper temperature. Turn the fritters after 1 minute and fry until they are golden brown, about 1 more minute. Using a slotted spoon, transfer the fritters to absorbent paper to drain. Continue until all the batter has been used.

Serve the fritters immediately, with one or both of the suggested sauces.

Gravlax with Mustard Cream

I have found very few home cooks willing to cure their own salmon, even though it is so very easy to do. My friend John Kramer, a professor at the local university, makes gravlax regularly, and it was his ease in doing so that got me started. And it is so wonderful, so bright and full of delicate good flavor, that it is a shame not to make it. Gravlax is a particularly easy dish for a party, because the work—and there's not much of that—comes mostly a few days before serving. It is traditionally served with sour cream, onions, and capers, but I enjoy the addition of some good Dijon mustard. It is also outstanding accompanied by salsas made with fruit, like mango or pineapple.

GRAVLAX:

2 salmon fillets, 10 to 14 ounces each, with skin intact

$1/4$ cup kosher salt

2 tablespoons granulated sugar

1 teaspoon crushed black peppercorns

$1/4$ cup framboise or tequila (optional)

sprigs of fresh dill (with no liqueur), rosemary (with framboise), or cilantro (with tequila)

FOR SERVING:

1 red onion, sliced paper-thin

2 tablespoons drained capers

1 lemon, cut into tiny wedges

Mustard Cream (page 186)

Crackers, toast triangles, or croutons

To prepare the gravlax, place one of the fillets, skin side down on a large platter with a deep lip or in a stainless-steel pan. Mix together the salt, sugar, and pepper. Sprinkle about half of the salt mixture over the salmon fillet, sprinkling more heavily on the thicker portion of the salmon and more lightly near the tail. Spread the mixture with your fingers so that it covers the entire surface. Repeat the process with the remaining salt mixture, so that you have a fairly heavy coating over the salmon. If using, quickly pour the framboise or tequila down the center of the fillet, add the herb sprigs, and place the second fillet on top, head to tail and skin side up. Loosely cover the salmon itself with plastic wrap.

Weight the salmon by covering it with a plate, a clean cutting board, a skillet, or other appropriate surface and placing a substantial weight on top. I use 2 heavy cast-iron platters, but a plate with a brick or 2 large full cans (say, of tomatoes) would work just as well. Refrigerate the salmon, turning it twice each day, once in the morning and once at the end of the day, lifting the 2 fillets together and turning the whole affair over. Baste with the juices that collect in the bottom of the container.

I find 3 days is the perfect curing time, although some cooks begin to use the salmon after 2 days of curing and others suggest as many as 5. When ready to serve, remove a fillet and place it skin side down on your work surface. Remove and discard the herb sprigs. Slice the salmon on the diagonal and very thinly, cutting only the amount you need. Return the rest to the refrigerator, covered, where it should keep well for another several days.

Serve the salmon in one of two fashions. Prepare a platter with the gravlax, onion, capers, and lemon wedges arranged around a small bowl of the Mustard Cream. Place the crackers or toasts in a basket on the side. Guests assemble their own servings. Or you can assemble each serving in the kitchen and place them on a serving tray.

Rock Shrimp with Rémoulade Sauce

Serves 4 to 8

Rock shrimp have a more delicate, sweeter flavor that I prefer over that of the larger shrimp and prawns that are more commonly served as appetizers. It may seem odd to pair these crustaceans with strawberries, but I have done it on countless occasions and with great success. Here, the slightly sweet tang of the sauce ties the whole dish together, making it an ideal appetizer or an excellent first course. You can, of course, use prawns instead of rock shrimp, with no adjustments necessary.

RÉMOULADE SAUCE:

1/4 lemon, cut into pieces

3 tablespoons ketchup

2 tablespoons Worcester-
shire sauce

2 tablespoons coarse-grain
mustard

2 tablespoons finely
minced onion

2 tablespoons finely
minced celery

2 tablespoons finely
minced whole green
onions

2 tablespoons finely
minced fresh Italian
parsley

1 tablespoon Dijon
mustard

1 tablespoon Tabasco
sauce

1 tablespoon white wine
vinegar

1 tablespoon minced
garlic

1/4 cup sour cream

3/4 cup homemade or
high-quality prepared
mayonnaise

1/2 teaspoon paprika

1/2 teaspoon kosher salt

1 pound rock shrimp or
unshelled medium
prawns

Olive oil

Salt and freshly ground
black pepper

1 lemon

1 fennel bulb, trimmed,
thinly sliced

1 bunch radishes, trimmed

1 basket strawberries
(optional)

Fresh Italian parsley
sprigs, for garnish

Make the sauce 1 to 2 days in advance, since it takes longer to prepare than the shrimp. Place all of the ingredients except the mayonnaise, paprika, and salt in a food processor and pulse until well combined and the lemon is finely chopped. Spoon the mayonnaise into a mixing bowl. Transfer the processed mixture to the bowl and fold it into the mayonnaise. Add the paprika and salt, taste, and adjust the seasonings. You will have about 1¾ cups. Cover and chill until ready to serve.

To prepare the rock shrimp, heat a small amount of olive oil in a heavy skillet over high heat. Add the shrimp a handful at a time (be careful not to crowd the pan), and sauté until they turn pink, about 2 minutes on each side. Do not overcook. Transfer the shrimp to a bowl or plate and season with salt, pepper, and a substantial squeeze of lemon juice. You may hold the cooked shrimp in the refrigerator for a few hours and serve them chilled or you may assemble the dish immediately after cooking the shrimp.

When ready to serve, spread the fennel over the surface of a serving platter, leaving room in the center for a bowl to hold the sauce. Arrange the strawberries, if used, around the edge of the platter and place the shrimp atop the fennel. Garnish with the radishes and parsley sprigs. Fill the bowl with the sauce, place on the platter, and serve.

Squash Broth with Broccoli Rabe, White Beans, & Curry Mustard Oil

Serves 4

A broth of winter squash extracts the sweet essence of these hearty vege-tables. The flavor is delicate, and ideal with the slight bitterness of the broccoli rabe and the creaminess of the white beans.

10 pounds cut up winter squash (Delicata, butter-nut, acorn, banana), stems discarded

2 medium or 1 large leek, carefully washed and sliced

3 quarts good, clear water (use spring water if your tap water is not great)

2 bunches broccoli rabe, trimmed and divided into stalks

1 cup small white beans, cooked until tender, and drained

About 4 teaspoons mus-tard oil infused with curry spices (see Note)

$\frac{1}{2}$ teaspoon cumin seed, toasted

Bake the squash in a 325°F oven until it is just tender, about 40 minutes. Make a broth by combining the baked squash, leeks, and water in a large stockpot. Simmer, covered, for about 1 hour. Strain the broth through several layers of cheesecloth, return it to the pan, and reduce it to about 6 cups. Strain the broth again and return it to the pan.

Meanwhile, place the broccoli rabe on a steamer rack over gently boiling water, cover, and steam until just tender, about 5 minutes. Divide the broccoli rabe and the white beans among 4 heated soup plates. Reheat the broth and ladle it over the vegetables. Drizzle each serving with about 1 teaspoon of mustard oil (a squeeze bottle makes this simple) and sprinkle a few cumin seeds over the soup. Serve immediately.

Note: To make a curry mustard oil, combine 1 cup mustard oil, 1 teaspoon cumin seeds, 2 to 3 whole cloves, 2 to 3 cardamom seeds, and 1 teaspoon curry powder. Let sit for several days and then strain through a fine-mesh sieve lined with cheesecloth. Store in the panty in a tightly capped bottle for up to three weeks.

Dal with Yogurt & Chutney

Serves 4 to 6

In the mid-seventies, I spent several months in India and came to love the simple foods of the countryside where I lived. My meals were made up primarily of a platter of cucumbers and tomatoes, a big bowl of rice, and a simple soup of either channa dal *(yellow split peas) or* masoor dal *(red lentils) spooned over the rice. I have been making a version of that dal in my own kitchen since my return, and I always find it evocative, refreshing, and delicious. My recipe deviates somewhat from what I was taught so long ago in India, but I believe it retains the authentic flavors of the region.*

1 cup red lentils or yellow split peas

6 to 8 cups water

1 onion, minced

3 tablespoons mustard oil

3 or 4 cloves garlic, minced

1 teaspoon brown mustard seeds

1 teaspoon grated, peeled fresh ginger

1 teaspoon ground cumin

$\frac{1}{2}$ teaspoon ground nutmeg

1 teaspoon ground cardamom

1 teaspoon ground tumeric

1 teaspoon cayenne pepper

Salt and freshly ground black pepper

2 cups cooked basmati rice (optional)

$\frac{1}{2}$ cup plain yogurt

Chutney

$\frac{1}{2}$ cup fresh cilantro leaves or 1 bunch sautéed coarsely chopped mustard greens

Pick through the lentils (or peas) and discard any stones or darkened lentils. Place the lentils in a heavy pot, add 6 cups of the water, and bring to a boil. Lower the heat, wait about 5 minutes, and then skim off the scum that forms on top.

While the lentils are cooking, sauté the onions in the mustard oil over medium heat until they are soft and transparent, about 15 minutes. Add the garlic and sauté for another 2 minutes. Add the seeds and spices (except the salt and black pepper) one at a time, stirring after each addition.

Stir the onion and spice mixture into the lentils and continue to cook until the lentils fall apart. I generally cook dal for about 1 hour, but the timing depends on the age of the lentils or the peas. They will continue to absorb water after cooking and frequently require additional water before serving. Taste the soup and season with salt and black pepper.

To serve the soup, place a scoop of rice, if using, into each bowl. Ladle the dal over the rice or simply into each bowl by itself. Garnish with a spoonful of yogurt and a spoonful of chutney. Top each serving with a sprinkling of cilantro leaves or some of the sautéed mustard greens.

Classic Southern Greens & Ham Hocks

Serves 8

Generally served as a side dish with fried or roasted chicken, ham, or black-eyed peas, I find greens and ham hocks also make a great soup and accompany it with corn bread. It is best in the cooler months, not only because it is hearty and warming, but because that's when mustard greens are at their best. All brassicas *thrive in cool weather.*

3 ham hocks, split
4 quarts water
4 large bunches of
   mustard greens

2 teaspoons freshly
   ground black pepper
Salt
$\frac{1}{4}$ cup apple cider vinegar
$\frac{1}{4}$ cup Tabasco sauce

Place the ham hocks in a large pot and add the water. Bring to a boil and skim off any foam. Reduce the heat and simmer the hocks for 1 hour, skimming off the foam as needed.

Meanwhile, trim the greens, removing any tough stems or yellowed leaves. Soak them briefly in warm water to clean them and transfer them to absorbent paper. Slice them crosswise into inch-wide strips. Add them to the ham hocks and cook 25 to 60 minutes. Younger mustard greens will cook more quickly than older, more mature greens.

Lift the ham hocks out of the liquid, pull the meat off the bones, and discard the bones. Return the meat to the pot, add the pepper, and taste the liquid. Add salt as needed; the amount will depend on how salty the ham hocks are, which varies greatly.

Mix together the vinegar and Tabasco sauce and add 1 tablespoon to the greens and ham hocks. Ladle the soup into bowls and serve the remaining pepper-vinegar mixture on the side.

VARIATION:
For a more substantial soup, add 2 pounds of cubed, un-peeled red potatoes along with the mustard greens.

Chicken Stew with Winter Squash & Mustard Greens

Serves 4 as a main course; 8 as a hearty first course

I love this soup on a blustery cold day. It is robust, delicious, and a little unusual in its use of squash and spices, which add an element of sweetness.

3 tablespoons pure olive oil

4 chicken thighs

4 chicken legs

Salt and freshly ground black pepper

2 red onions, cut into ½-inch squares

8 cloves garlic, minced

1 or 2 fresh jalapeño peppers, minced

¼ teaspoon ground nutmeg

¼ teaspoon ground cardamom

½ teaspoon ground cumin

1 cup cooked chick-peas

1 cup unpeeled waxy potatoes, cut into ½-inch squares

1 cup ½-inch-cubed, peeled winter squash (butternut or Delicata)

6 cups homemade chicken stock

½ pound mustard greens, trimmed and cut into ½-inch wide strips

¼ cup chopped cilantro leaves

Heat 2 tablespoons of the olive oil in a large, heavy pot. Season the chicken parts with salt and pepper and sauté them until golden brown on all sides. Remove the chicken from the pot.

Add the onions to the pot and sauté until transparent. Add the garlic and jalapeño peppers and sauté another 2 minutes. Add the spices, chick-peas, potatoes, and squash. Sauté 2 minutes, add the chicken stock, and return the chicken to the pot. Simmer until the potatoes and squash are just tender and the chicken is cooked through, about 15 minutes.

Meanwhile, sauté the mustard greens in the remaining tablespoon of olive oil until they are just limp. Add the greens to the soup. Taste, and adjust seasoning with salt and pepper.

To serve, place 2 pieces of chicken in each warmed soup bowl and ladle the broth and vegetables over the chicken. Top each serving with some of the chopped cilantro.

Cream of Mustard Soup with Four Variations

Serves 6

Consider this soup a master recipe. I recommend using it as a base for one of the variations. Its roots are old, indeed, going back to the earliest cookbooks of France when mustard was used with great frequency. I have added aromatics that were not a part of the original recipe.

6 tablespoons butter
1 leek, white part only, thinly sliced
1 small yellow onion, chopped
1 small carrot, peeled and thinly sliced
1 shallot, minced
3 cloves garlic, minced
6 tablespoons all-purpose flour
3 cups homemade chicken stock, heated
1 ½ cups half-and-half or milk, scalded
1 small bouquet garni (fresh oregano, thyme, Italian parsley, marjoram)
½ cup heavy cream
2 egg yolks
¼ cup Dijon mustard
½ teaspoon white pepper
Salt
1 tablespoon snipped fresh chives

Melt the butter in a heavy pot and sauté the vegetables over medium heat until they are soft and the onion is translucent. Stir in the flour and cook, stirring, for an additional 5 minutes. Whisk in the chicken stock and the half-and-half or milk, add the bouquet garni, and simmer, uncovered, for 45 minutes.

Strain the sauce, return it to a clean soup pot, add the heavy cream, heat to a boil, and then reduce the heat. Stir a tiny bit of the hot soup into the egg yolks, and then a little more and a little more again, until the egg yolks are quite warm, and then whisk them into the soup. Very slowly bring the soup back to a boil and remove it from the heat immediately. Stir in the mustard and the pepper, taste, and add salt as necessary. The amount of salt you need will be determined by how much salt is in the mustard.

Ladle into soup bowls and top each serving with a sprinkling of chives.

VARIATIONS:

1. Cut enough broccoli florets to make 3 cups of bite-size pieces, and steam until just done. Either add them to the soup just before serving or place them in the bowls and ladle the soup over them.

2. Top each serving with several strips of julienned cooked chicken meat.

3. Cut 1 pound of asparagus tips into 1½-inch pieces, steam them, and divide them among the soup bowls before adding the soup.

4. Sauté 2 cups of thinly sliced scallions (green part included) in butter until they are just soft. Add them to the soup along with the mustard. Garnish each serving with 2 tablespoons of chopped, peeled cucumber and the chives.

Beef-Barley Soup with Mustard

Serves 4 to 6

I love the hearty comfort this soup provides in the middle of a winter storm. There is a subtle spiciness provided by the mustard that makes the combination of flavors rich and compelling.

1 cup barley

2 tablespoons pure olive oil

1 yellow onion, diced

5 or 6 cloves garlic, minced

1 pound beef (chuck roast or stew meat), cut into 1-inch cubes

6 cups homemade beef stock

1 can (28 ounces) tomatoes or 2 pounds fresh tomatoes, peeled, seeded, and chopped

Bouquet garni (fresh basil, sage, oregano, thyme, and Italian parsley)

1 pound waxy potatoes, cut into medium to large dice

1 tablespoon soy sauce

2 tablespoons hot mustard flour (or Colman's dry mustard)

Salt and freshly ground black pepper

Soak 1 cup barley in water for at least 2 hours but no more than 3. In a large, heavy pot, sauté the onion in the olive oil until it is transparent. Add the garlic and the beef and sauté 5 minutes. Add the beef stock, tomatoes, and bouquet garni and simmer over low heat for 30 minutes.

Drain and rinse the barley and add it to the soup, along with the potatoes and soy sauce. Simmer for another 30 minutes. Mix the mustard flour with an equal amount of cold water and then stir it into the soup. Remove from the heat, lift out the bouquet garni, and season to taste with salt and plenty of black pepper.

Linguine with Salmon, Red Peppers, & Broccoli Rabe

Serves 4

Broccoli rabe is generally included in the same brassica *subgroup as standard broccoli because its tiny yellow florets somewhat resemble those of broccoli. It is actually a member of the turnip subgroup, but it is often called Italian mustard, hence its inclusion here. Regardless of the accuracy of its classification, it is a cousin of the true mustards rather than a closer relative. And, most important, it is one of the tastiest of the bitter greens. The flavors of this dish—sweet from the salmon and the peppers, bright and bitter from the broccoli rabe, tart from the citrus—blend beautifully into a light main dish, perfect in warm weather. Although the dish can be made without the bread crumbs, the flavorful crunch they contribute makes them worth the extra effort.*

1 pound salmon fillet
10 to 12 tablespoons light
   extra virgin olive oil
   (see Note)
Juice of 1 lemon
2 red sweet peppers
2 bunches (about 1 pound
   each) young broccoli
   rabe
3 green onions

6 ounces dried linguine,
   or 8 ounces fresh
   linquine
2 tablespoons fresh,
   snipped chives
Salt and freshly ground
   black pepper
1 cup Mustard Bread
   Crumbs (page 193)

Remove the skin and any bones from the salmon and slice it into thin strips. Toss it with 2 or 3 tablespoons of the olive oil and half the lemon juice. Set aside to marinate for at least 30 minutes, but no more than an hour or so.

Roast, peel, and seed the peppers and cut them into medium julienne. Set aside. Trim the broccoli rabe and separate into stalks. Heat about 3 tablespoons of the olive oil in a heavy skillet over medium heat. Add the broccoli rabe, cover, lower the heat, and cook it slowly until tender, 30 to 40 minutes.

Meanwhile, trim the green onions, leaving about 3 inches of the green, cut them into small rounds, and set them aside.

When the broccoli rabe is about done, have a pot of rapidly boiling water ready. If you are using dried pasta, begin to cook it now. If you are using fresh pasta, wait and start cooking it and the salmon at the same time. In a separate skillet, sauté the green onions in a small amount of the olive oil until they are soft. Add the roasted peppers and heat them through.

Place the green onions, peppers, and broccoli rabe in a warmed serving bowl. In the remaining olive oil, sauté the salmon very quickly, for just 1 or 2 minutes. Drain the pasta well and add it to the vegetable mixture. Add the salmon to the pasta and squeeze the remaining lemon juice over. Toss lightly with the chives, season with salt and pepper, top with the bread crumbs, and serve immediately.

Note: The flavor of the olive oil is important to this dish. You will get the best results if you use a late-harvest golden oil from Liguria. If this type is unavailable, a fruity green olive oil is the second best choice.

Macaroni & Cheese with Mustard Greens

Serves 4 to 6 as a side dish; 3 to 4 as a main course

This dish is hearty and flavorful enough to be the centerpiece of a winter's meal. Add some crisp salad greens and good bread and everyone will be well fed. It is also an excellent accompaniment to simple roasted meats and poultry, especially chicken. It is very versatile as well. Swiss chard can be substituted for the mustard greens, and vegetarians can enjoy it by substituting a little more olive oil for the pancetta.

1/4 pound pancetta or bacon, cut into strips 1/2 inch wide
1 tablespoon olive oil
2 cloves garlic, peeled
1 pound mustard greens, chopped
1/2 pound small dried pasta (salad macaroni, tripolini, or rotini)
2 teaspoons hot mustard flour (or Colman's dry mustard)
1 tablespoon Tabasco sauce
1 can (12 ounces) evaporated milk, or 1 cup milk plus 1/2 cup heavy cream
2 eggs, beaten
1 teaspoon freshly ground black pepper
1 pound sharp Cheddar cheese, grated
Mustard Bread Crumbs (page 193)

In a heavy skillet, sauté the *pancetta* in the olive oil until it is just barely crisp. If using bacon, omit the olive oil. Transfer the *pancetta* from the skillet to absorbent paper. Pour off all but 2 tablespoons of the pan drippings (there will be barely that much if using the *pancetta*). Add the mustard greens to the pan, cover, and cook over medium heat, about 5 minutes. Shake the pan frequently to prevent sticking. When the greens have wilted, remove the pan from the heat and set it aside.

Cook the pasta according to package directions until not quite done. Meanwhile, make a paste with the mustard flour and Tabasco sauce, stir it into the milk, and add the eggs and black pepper. Fold in two thirds of the cheese and combine the mixture with the drained pasta. Fold in the rest of the cheese, and pour half the mixture into a heavy 2-quart baking dish. Toss the mustard greens with the *pancetta* or bacon, spread them over the surface of the pasta, and top them with the remaining pasta mixture. Spread enough of the bread crumbs to evenly coat the surface, cover, and bake in a 350°F oven for 30 minutes, uncovering for the last 10 minutes. Serve immediately.

Mustard Frittata with Potatoes & Asparagus

Serves 4

A properly made frittata is more than just an open-faced omelet, as it is sometimes called. A frittata has a creamier texture and is really another thing altogether. It is an excellent main course for breakfast, brunch, or lunch, and can be varied to incorporate whatever seasonal vegetables or herbs you have available. This version is my favorite, especially when I make it with tiny Yellow Finn potatoes from my garden.

4 small, waxy potatoes (Yellow Finn, Rose Fir, or new red), unpeeled, boiled until just tender
6 eggs
3 tablespoons plus 1 teaspoon Dijon mustard, plus additional mustard for serving
1 teaspoon kosher salt, plus salt to taste
Freshly ground black pepper
2 teaspoons butter
1 pound asparagus
1 teaspoon brown sugar
3 tablespoons balsamic vinegar, plus vinegar for brushing on top
½ cup extra virgin olive oil

Slice the potatoes into very thin rounds. Break the eggs into a large mixing bowl, add the 3 tablespoons mustard, and whisk together vigorously. Season the eggs with the 1 teaspoon salt and several turns of black pepper.

Melt the butter in a 10-inch cast-iron skillet over high heat. Make sure the butter coats the entire pan. Spread the potatoes over the surface, pour the eggs in, and leave over the heat for 1 minute. Transfer the pan to a 275°F oven and bake until the eggs are set, about 12 to 14 minutes. Be sure not to overcook.

While the frittata is cooking, trim the asparagus and cook until just tender. Rinse the asparagus under cold water, drain, and set aside.

Whisk together the remaining teaspoon mustard, the brown sugar, the 3 tablespoons balsamic vinegar, and the olive oil. Taste the vinaigrette and add salt and pepper.

Remove the pan from the oven, brush the surface of the frittata with a very thin coating of balsamic vinegar, and top it with a few more turns of black pepper. Let the frittata rest for 5 minutes and then remove it from the pan, loosening it with a knife if it sticks. Arrange the asparagus spears on a large platter or on 4 individual plates and drizzle a small amount of the vinaigrette over the spears. Carefully slice the frittata into strips about ⅛ inch wide and 3 inches long, and add them, randomly, to the plates or platter. Serve immediately, with additional mustard and the remaining vinaigrette on the side.

VARIATIONS:

HERB FRITTATA: Omit the potatoes. Add 2 tablespoons of chopped fresh herbs (oregano, marjoram, chives, thyme, summer savory) and ¾ cup freshly grated Romano cheese to the egg mixture and cook as directed.

LEEK FRITTATA: Sauté the white part, sliced, of 2 leeks in butter, add it to the egg mixture, and cook as directed.

Gruyère Soufflé

A soufflé adds a special touch to a meal, a tenderness evoked by the delicate nature of the soufflé itself. But do not confuse a soufflé's delicacy with difficulty. Soufflés are really quite easy to make, and although they are beautiful when we first pull them from the oven, rising high as they do over the rim of the dish like a golden cloud, their almost immediate fall is not a sign of failure. Soufflés collapse on their own; it is in their nature, as is their delicious taste.

1 cup heavy cream
1 cup half-and-half
5 ounces Gruyère cheese
4 egg yolks
3 to 4 tablespoons extra-forte Dijon mustard
Salt to taste, plus 1 teaspoon salt
Freshly ground black pepper

1 tablespoon butter
1 ½ teaspoons hot mustard flour (or Colman's dry mustard)
5 egg whites
Boiling water, as needed
Dijon Pear Sauce (page 192)
1 ripe pear

Place the cream and half-and-half in a heavy saucepan over medium heat and reduce by nearly half, being careful not to let the mixture boil over. Remove from the heat and let cool. Grate the Gruyère cheese and set it aside. Beat together the egg yolks and mustard and add them to the reduced cream. Add the grated cheese, stir to blend it in, and season to taste with salt and pepper. This part of the soufflé can be made in advance and set aside. Refrigerate if you will not use it within 30 minutes, but bring the mixture to room temperature before proceeding with the soufflé.

Preheat oven to 350°F. Butter a 1-quart soufflé dish. Stir together the 1 teaspoon salt and the mustard flour. Place the mixture in the soufflé dish and then shake the dish until it has coated the bottom and sides. Shake out any excess and set the soufflé dish aside.

Beat the egg whites until stiff but not dry; gently and quickly fold them into the cream mixture. Using a rubber spatula to scrape the bowl, pour the soufflé mixture into the soufflé dish and place it in a large baking dish or pan. Pour boiling water to a depth of 2 inches into the baking dish.

Bake for 20 minutes; check carefully to see if it is done. The soufflé should have risen well above the dish and be a warm, toasty brown. Remove from the oven and serve immediately, with sliced pears and the Dijon Pear Sauce on the side.

VARIATION:
Quickly sauté the pears in butter before serving them.

Leek & Mustard Tart

Serves 6

I love leeks, and this creamy tart is rich with their flavor, which blends wonderfully with the mustard. Serve this tart as the main course of a light lunch, brunch, or summer dinner, accompanied by a delicate chilled soup, perhaps, and a salad with lots of crunch in it.

3 tablespoons butter
5 cups sliced (¼ inch thick) leeks, with 2 inches of green stems
½ cup water
Salt and freshly ground pepper
3 eggs
1 ½ cups heavy cream

¼ cup Dijon mustard, plus additional mustard for brushing on tart shell
4 ounces chèvre
2 tablespoons snipped fresh chives
1 partially baked 10-inch tart shell

Melt the butter in a heavy skillet. Add the leeks and sauté for 5 minutes. Add the water and simmer until it evaporates. Season to taste with salt and pepper and remove from the heat. Mix together the eggs, heavy cream, the ¼ cup mustard, and the *chèvre*. Brush the surface of the tart shell with the additional Dijon. Spread the leeks evenly in the shell. Pour the custard mixture over the leeks and sprinkle with the chives.

Bake the tart in a preheated 350°F oven until it is firm and beginning to turn golden brown, about 30 minutes.

VARIATION:

Omit the butter. Sauté 4 strips bacon until just crisp. Transfer the bacon to absorbent paper, then sauté the leeks in the bacon drippings. Crumble the bacon and set it aside. Substitute ½ cup medium-dry white wine for the water. Proceed as directed, but sprinkle the bacon over the surface of the custard before baking. Serve at room temperature.

# Leek Strudel

I am particularly fond of vegetable strudels and find that everyone I serve them to is quite pleased by them as well. Because leeks and mustard are such good companions, I developed this version of vegetable strudel to accent the delicious results of their marriage.

DOUGH:

1 cup unsalted butter
8 ounces cream cheese
2½ cups unbleached flour

1 teaspoon kosher salt
¼ cup heavy cream

FILLING:

2 tablespoons olive oil or
  butter
2 pounds leeks, trimmed
  and sliced, including
  about 2 inches of green
  tops
2 sweet onions (Walla
  Walla, Vidalia, Maui, or
  sweet torpedo), sliced
3 to 6 cloves garlic,
  minced
Salt and freshly ground
  black pepper

2 tablespoons Dijon mus-
  tard, plus additional
  mustard for serving
4 ounces cheese (Gruyère,
  doux de montagne,
  Fontina, or St. George)
  (see Note), grated or
  sliced
1 tablespoon snipped
  fresh chives
1 egg white, lightly beaten

To make the dough, combine the butter and cream cheese in an electric mixer until smooth. Sift together the flour and salt and gradually add to the cheese mixture. Add the cream, mix well, and transfer the dough to a floured surface. Form the dough into a ball, place in plastic wrap, and chill for 1 hour. The dough can be made up to 2 days in advance; remove it from the refrigerator 30 minutes before rolling it out on a floured surface.

To make the filling, heat the olive oil or butter in a heavy skillet. Sauté the leeks and onions until limp. Add the garlic and sauté for another 2 minutes. Season to taste with salt and pepper and set aside to cool.

To assemble the strudel, roll out the chilled dough into a rectangle measuring 10 by 12 inches. Brush the surface of the dough with the mustard. Place the onion and leek filling down the center and top it evenly with the cheese. Sprinkle the chives over the cheese. Fold the pastry over to form a long cylinder and seal the edges with egg white. Brush the top of the pastry with egg white and sprinkle with salt. Using a sharp knife, cut crosswise through the top of the pastry at 1½-inch intervals. Transfer the strudel to a baking sheet.

Bake the strudel in a 400°F oven until it is lightly golden, 20 to 25 minutes. Remove from the oven, let rest for 10 minutes, and then slice. Serve warm with Dijon mustard on the side.

Note: St. George cheese is a semisoft Portuguese-style cheese made in Sonoma County, California, and available by mail order.

Deviled Crab Cakes

Makes about eight 3-inch cakes; serves 4

In The Chesapeake Bay Crab Cookbook, *John Shields offers several recipes combining mustard and crab, a culinary liaison of long and delicious duration. From soft-shell crabs slathered with Dijon, breaded, and panfried in butter, to a half-dozen variations on crab cakes, his recipes are spirited, easy to prepare, and, well, really, really good. Similar to John's recipes, this version features mustard in both the crab cake itself and in the sauce that accompanies it. Unlike the traditional crab cakes of Chesapeake Bay, these cakes are bound with cream rather than mayonnaise. It is a wonderful version and has become a tradition in my home on New Year's Eve (and New Year's Day, too, if we have any left over).*

3 tablespoons butter
¼ cup minced yellow onion
1 or 2 fresh jalapeño peppers, seeded and minced
⅔ cup finely chopped celery
3 eggs, well beaten
¾ cup heavy cream, partially whipped until thick
2 tablespoons Dijon mustard, or more to taste
2 tablespoons fresh lemon juice

1 tablespoon chopped fresh Italian parsley
About 3 cups fresh bread crumbs or Mustard Bread Crumbs (page 193)
3 cups fresh crab meat
Salt and freshly ground black pepper
Jalapeño-Cilantro Mustard (page 177)
Lime wedges
Chopped fresh cilantro

Melt 1 tablespoon of the butter in a sauté pan. Add the onion and sauté until transparent. Add the jalapeños and the celery and sauté for another 5 minutes. Remove from the heat and set aside to cool briefly.

Add the vegetables to the beaten eggs and fold in the cream and then the mustard, lemon juice, and parsley. Add 1 cup of the bread crumbs, carefully fold in the crab, taste, and season with salt and pepper. Cover and chill for two hours before making the crab cakes.

To make the cakes, heat the remaining 2 tablespoons of butter in a heavy skillet until foamy. If the crab mixture seems a little too moist, add another ½ cup to 1 cup of the remaining bread crumbs and form cakes about 3 inches across. Dust the cakes lightly with the bread crumbs and sauté them—making sure not to crowd them in the skillet—for about 4 minutes before turning and sautéing for an additional 3 to 4 minutes. They should be lightly browned. Transfer the cakes to serving plates, 2 per serving, and top each one with a spoonful of the mustard. Garnish with a wedge of lime and some chopped cilantro.

Scallops in Lemon-Mustard Sauce

Serves 4

Scallops are best when they are cooked quickly and lightly, so that they remain tender and don't develop an unpleasant, overly fishy flavor, which they do with overcooking. So be sure to get the scallops off the heat and served the moment they are done. Accompany them with a simple pasta—linguine is perfect—and a green vegetable. Green beans and spinach are both good.

1 pound bay scallops or calico scallops
2 tablespoons all-purpose flour
1 teaspoon hot mustard flour (or Colman's dry mustard)
$\frac{1}{2}$ teaspoon salt, plus salt to taste
$\frac{1}{2}$ teaspoon white pepper
2 tablespoons butter
$\frac{1}{4}$ cup white wine
Juice of 1 lemon
1 cup heavy cream
1 tablespoon Dijon mustard
$\frac{1}{2}$ teaspoon lemon zest, finely grated
Freshly ground black pepper

Clean the scallops, if necessary, and pat them dry. Mix together the flour, mustard flour, salt, and white pepper. Toss the scallops in the mixture and shake them in a colander or sieve.

Melt the butter over medium heat in a heavy skillet and when it is foamy, add the scallops. Sauté quickly, shaking the pan so that they do not burn, until they are done, about 5 minutes. Do not overcook. Transfer the scallops to a plate and cover to keep warm.

Deglaze the pan with the white wine and reduce until there is only about a tablespoon left. Add half the lemon juice, reduce again by half, and add the cream. Reduce the cream by about one third, remove the pan from the heat, add the mustard and lemon zest, taste, add salt and black pepper, and the remaining lemon juice if the sauce needs more tartness. Toss the scallops with the cream sauce and serve immediately.

Trout with Mushrooms & Mustard Bread Crumbs

Serves 4

I love the delicate flesh of trout and often I prefer them prepared very simply, with just a squeeze of lemon and a little salt. Sometimes, however, a more elaborate preparation is in order and then a dish like this is ideal.

4 small rainbow trout (8 to 10 ounces each)
1 pound mushrooms (commercial, shiitake, or a mix of wild mushrooms)
2 tablespoons butter
1 small shallot, minced
3 cloves garlic, minced
Salt and freshly ground black pepper

3 tablespoons minced Italian parsley
2 tablespoons snipped chives
3 cups Mustard Bread Crumbs (page 193)
2 tablespoons Dijon mustard
2 lemons
Mustard butter (page 185)

Rinse the trout and pat them dry. Clean the mushrooms, remove any hard stems, and slice them (if they are a mix of wild mushrooms, break them into medium-sized pieces).

Melt the butter in a heavy skillet over medium heat and add the shallots. Sauté until soft. Add the garlic, sauté for 2 minutes, and add the mushrooms. Lower the heat, cover the pan, and simmer the mushrooms until they are limp, about 15 minutes.

While the mushrooms are cooking, salt and pepper the cavities of the trout. Stir 1 tablespoon each of Italian parsley and chives into the bread crumbs and fill the cavity of each trout with about ½ cup of crumb mixture. (You should have about 1 cup of the bread crumbs left.) Stir the remaining parsley and chives and the Dijon mustard into the mushrooms and season them with salt and pepper. Place the mushrooms in a shallow baking dish just large enough to hold the 4 trout. Lay the trout on top of the mushrooms, squeeze the juice of one lemon over the trout, and dot each one with about 2 teaspoons of mustard butter. Top the trout with the remaining bread crumbs. Bake in a preheated 375°F oven until the fish is just done, about 15 to 20 minutes, depending on the size of the trout.

Cut the remaining lemon into wedges. Garnish each serving with a wedge of lemon and a bit of Mustard Butter.

Fillet of Sole with Asparagus & Mustard

Serves 4

The preparation for these fish fillets is so easy that a recipe is barely required. It is a casual dish, one that can be prepared very quickly and is quite low in fat.

1 pound asparagus, trimmed
4 sole fillets, Rex or Petrale, 4 to 6 ounces each

Salt and freshly ground pepper
Honey-Ginger Mustard (page 175)
2 cups Mustard Bread Crumbs (page 193)

Steam the asparagus until it is just barely tender, about 7 to 8 minutes, and hold in cold water. Season the sole fillets with salt and pepper. Brush one side of each fillet with the mustard, lay 4 or 5 spears of asparagus across the fillet, and roll the fillet up, so that it forms a little blanket around the asparagus. Brush the outside of the fillets with additional mustard, roll them in the bread crumbs, and place them, seam side down, in a baking dish. Bake in a 350°F oven until the fish is tender and flaky, about 15 to 20 minutes. Serve immediately, with more mustard on the side.

VARIATION:

When asparagus is out of season, make this dish with zucchini. Cut the ends from a zucchini and cut it lengthwise into 4 strips. Parboil the strips for about a minute, drain them, lay one on each mustard-brushed fillet, roll them up, and proceed as directed.

Salmon with Asparagus & Dijon Hollandaise

Serves 4 to 6

So well do these three ingredients go together that the dish is nearly a classic, served with subtle variations in restaurants and home kitchens throughout the country and beyond. It can be as casual or as elegant as you like. For a simple, summer party, grill or poach a whole salmon and let your guests serve themselves. Another time you might want to quickly broil salmon steaks and serve them atop the sauce, with the fresh aspara-

gus spread out across the plate like an elegant Japanese fan. However you choose to present this spectacular combination of flavors, you and your guests will be delighted.

4 to 6 salmon fillets, 6 to 8 ounces each, or 1 small salmon, about 4 pounds
1 pound asparagus, preferably white
½ cup plus 2 tablespoons butter
3 egg yolks

1 tablespoon extra-forte Dijon mustard
1 tablespoon Champagne vinegar or fresh lemon juice
1 tablespoon hot water
¼ teaspoon kosher salt
Pinch of white pepper

To grill the salmon, have coals prepared and settled down to a moderate glow. Melt the butter until it is foamy, brush the salmon with a little butter and place on the grill. Grill, turning once, until just tender, about 5 to 7 minutes per side for fillets and 10 to 18 minutes per whole salmon. Steam the asparagus about 6 to 7 minutes and keep it warm.

Meanwhile, place the egg yolks, mustard, vinegar or lemon juice, hot water, salt, and pepper in a blender container. Process the mixture for 30 seconds. Slowly drizzle in the hot melted butter, continuing to process the entire time. Hold the sauce until the salmon is done by placing the blender container in a bowl of medium-hot water. (It can also be held in a Thermos that you have first warmed with boiling water.) The sauce must never reach a temperature of 180°F or it will break.

To serve, arrange the salmon and asparagus side by side on a serving platter or individual plates. Spoon the sauce over both and serve immediately.

Grilled Tuna with Black Beans & Jalapeño-Cilantro Mustard

Serves 4

This is a simple combination of bright, contrasting flavors. I particularly enjoy the cool spark contributed by the pineapple and love this dish on a hot night. It is something I frequently make for myself when I am eating alone; the portions are easy to scale down. Grilled poblano peppers stuffed with chèvre make an excellent accompaniment.

4 ounces black beans, soaked overnight in water to cover and drained
1 whole jalapeño pepper, scored
1 small yellow onion
1 celery stalk, cut in half
4 cloves garlic, peeled
Salt and freshly ground black pepper
Jalapeño-Cilantro Mustard (page 177)
4 tuna steaks, about 6 ounces each
3 tablespoons fresh lime juice
1 pineapple
Sprigs of fresh cilantro

Place the beans in a heavy pot with water to cover them by 2 inches. Add the jalapeño pepper, onion, celery, and whole garlic cloves. Bring to a boil, reduce the heat to low, and simmer the beans until they are very tender. The time will depend on the dryness of the beans; some take longer than others. Remove from the heat and discard the aromatics. Season with salt and pepper and set aside.

Brush the tuna steaks with a thin coating of the mustard and let sit for 30 minutes. Peel, quarter lengthwise, and core the pineapple. Chop one quarter into medium dice, and slice another quarter into slices for garnish; reserve the remaining half for another recipe. Prepare a fire in a charcoal grill or preheat a broiler. Place the tuna steaks on the grill rack or on the broiler pan and cook until just done but still quite pink through the center. It will take just 4 to 5 minutes per side, maximum.

While the tuna is cooking, warm the beans and 4 serving plates and heat the tortillas, timing carefully so that the tortillas will be hot when served. Place a tortilla on each warmed plate and top it with a generous serving of black beans and a spoonful or two of pineapple. When the tuna is done, transfer a steak to each of the serving plates, laying it off center on top of the beans and pineapple. Top each serving with a sprig of cilantro, a spoonful of the mustard, and a small spoonful of the pineapple. For a more decorative touch, have the mustard in a squeeze bottle fitted with a top whose opening is larger than normal. Add the mustard in a decorative slash across the tuna, pineapple, and tortilla. Garnish each plate with a slice or two of pineapple and a sprig of cilantro and serve immediately.

Braised Artichokes with Crab & Mustard Cream Dressing

Serves 4

Just days before I completed the manuscript for this book, my dear friend Anna Cherney—who turns ninety-three this year—called me. She was a little bored, I think, and I told her I'd come by and fix dinner for the two of us. I worked for a few more hours, ran to the store where I got one of the last crabs of the season, and headed to her house. I picked the crab from the shell while the artichokes cooked, sliced some fresh strawberries, added stalks of spring asparagus to our plates and—voilà!—dinner was ready in less than 30 minutes. Anna loved it; and I was happy to take some time out to visit with a special friend and very pleased that these flavor combinations worked as well as I hoped they would.

2 large or 4 small artichokes

2 tablespoons olive oil

1 lemon

About 2 cups homemade chicken stock or water, at the boil

1 cup sour cream

1 teaspoon prepared creamy horseradish

⅓ cup Dijon mustard

2 tablespoons tomato paste

2 teaspoons granulated sugar

2 teaspoons Tabasco sauce

Cooked crab meat of 1 medium or 2 small crabs, with leg meat set aside

1 tablespoon snipped fresh chives

½ cup Kalamata olives; 2 hard-boiled eggs, cut into wedges; and/or 2 tablespoons drained capers for garnish

Trim the artichokes, cut them in half lengthwise, and place them cut side up in a heavy, ovenproof dish with a lid. Drizzle the olive oil over the artichokes and then squeeze the juice of half the lemon over them. Add the hot chicken stock or water to the dish so that it comes about halfway up the sides of the artichokes. Cover tightly and bake in a 350°F oven until they are tender, about 25 minutes; do not overcook. (The artichokes may also be steamed on the top of the stove.)

Meanwhile, make the dressing by mixing together until smooth the sour cream, horseradish, mustard, tomato paste, sugar, Tabasco sauce, and juice of the remaining half lemon. Chill until ready to serve.

When the artichokes are done, remove them from the pan and let cool until they are easy to handle. Scoop out the chokes and trim away any small, sharp leaves. Divide

the artichokes among 4 serving plates and fill each artichoke with the body meat of the crab. Top with two tablespoons of the dressing and divide the crab legs among the servings, placing them on top of the dressing. Sprinkle the crab with the chives. Add any or all of the garnishes to the plates and serve immediately. Pass the remaining dressing.

VARIATION:

Instead of using artichokes, serve the crab with the same dressing on a bed of avocado and pear slices that have been drizzled with the juice of half the lemon.

Polenta with Sausages, Apples, & Mustard Greens

Serves 4 to 6

If they are available to you, consider decorating the table with a bouquet of field mustard and apple blossoms. If vegetarians will be part of your dinner, serve the sausages separately from the polenta, not on top, and sauté the apples in a separate skillet. The resulting sauce won't be quite as flavorful, but everyone will be well fed.

4 to 5 cups water
2 teaspoons kosher salt
1 cup polenta (see Note)
5 teaspoons hot mustard
   flour, mixed with 2
   tablespoons water

4 tablespoons butter
3 1/2 ounces dry Jack
   cheese or other hard
   cheese, grated (about
   1 1/2 cups)

2 pounds chicken-apple
　　sausages or other
　　sausages of choice
Dry white wine, to cover
　　(optional)

2 tart-sweet apples,
　　peeled, cored, and cut
　　into $\frac{1}{4}$-inch-thick
　　rounds
1 quart young mustard
　　greens

Place 4 cups of the water in a large, heavy pot. Add the salt and whisk in the polenta. Place the pot over medium heat and bring slowly to a boil, stirring steadily. When the mixture begins to boil, reduce the heat. Simmer the polenta, stirring constantly, until the mixture begins to thicken, about 5 minutes. Once it has thickened, stir every couple of minutes for another 5 or 6 minutes. Add half of the mustard-water mixture and 2 tablespoons of the butter and stir well. Taste the polenta and if it is still grainy and hard, simmer for another 5 minutes, stirring constantly. The polenta should be fairly thick, but thin enough to fall from a spoon. If it is too thick, add the remaining 1 cup water, $\frac{1}{4}$ cup at a time. When the polenta is done, add the cheese and stir until it melts. The mixture should pour easily at this point. Place in a large shallow serving dish and place in a 200°F oven to keep warm while preparing the rest of the dish.

You can begin to prepare the sausages while you are cooking the polenta, if you like. Place the sausages in a heavy skillet and cover with water or a dry white wine. Simmer over medium heat, turning the sausages once, until the liquid evaporates; then brown the sausages evenly on all sides. Arrange the sausages over the polenta and keep warm in the oven.

Melt the remaining 2 tablespoons butter in the same skillet over medium heat and sauté the apples until they are just barely tender. Arrange over the polenta and sausages. Have the mustard greens nearby in a large bowl. Stir the remaining mustard-water mixture into the pan drippings, add a small amount of water or white wine, and deglaze the pan over medium heat. Add the greens and toss until they are just wilted. Place the greens on top of the polenta, sausages, and apples and serve immediately.

Note: Polenta is a coarsely ground cornmeal, and I believe it is worth the effort to find it. I don't recommend substituting regular cornmeal; the texture is quite inferior to true polenta.

Chicken with
Soft Polenta & Broccoli Rabe

Serves 4

This is one of those dishes that doesn't really need a recipe, a winning combination that requires that you just not mess with it too much. Use a free-range chicken, if available, as it will taste better than most commercial chickens. If you want to jazz it up a bit, coat the chicken in some good Dijon mustard instead of the olive oil and stir a little mustard flour mixed with cold water into the polenta. Or drizzle the final dish with about a quarter cup of the best extra virgin olive oil you can get your hands on. Yum.

1 chicken, about 4½ to 5
   pounds, cut into serving
   pieces
Extra virgin olive oil
Salt and freshly ground
   black pepper
1 lemon

2 cups chicken stock
3 cups water
1 cup polenta
1 teaspoon kosher salt
1 tablespoon butter
2 bunches broccoli rabe,
   about 1¼ pounds each

Rub the chicken pieces with some olive oil and season them with salt and pepper. Squeeze the juice of the lemon over them and let sit for 1 hour. Place the chicken pieces on a baking rack in a good roasting pan and bake in a 400°F oven until done, 30 to 50 minutes, depending on how you like your chicken.

About 20 minutes or so before the chicken will be ready, combine 1 cup of the chicken stock, which should be cold, and all the water in a heavy pot. Whisk in the polenta, place the pot over medium heat, and add the salt and butter. Stir constantly until the polenta slowly comes to a boil and begins to thicken, about 5 minutes. Lower the heat and stir occasionally while it cooks another 5 or 6 minutes. Meanwhile, steam the broccoli rabe in the remaining chicken stock and keep it warm.

When the chicken is done, remove it from the oven and place it on a warm plate. Over low, stove-top heat, deglaze the roasting pan with the cooking liquid from the broccoli rabe.

Pour the polenta into a large serving dish, arrange the chicken and the broccoli rabe on top, and pour the pan juices over it all. Serve immediately.

Chicken Breasts Marinated in Mustard Oil with Radishes, Preserved Lemons, & Orzo

Serves 4

Madeleine Kamman deserves credit for this recipe. I came across her version of it on a recipe flyer from Napa Valley Mustard Company promoting their mustard oil. I was drawn to the light and delicate flavors of the lemon and the radishes, and, after experimenting, decided to add my own touch with orzo and preserved lemons, which I was making at the time. This is a particularly refreshing dish, perfect on a hot summer day. If mustard oil is unavailable, use a delicate extra virgin olive oil, one from France or a late-harvest Ligurian oil, and add a tablespoon of white mustard seeds to the marinade.

2 whole chicken breasts, boned, halved, skinned, and trimmed of all fat
1 clove garlic, crushed
6 tablespoons lemon juice
3/4 cup mustard oil
2 bunches fresh radishes, plus 4 small radishes, trimmed with stems on, for garnish
4 ounces dried orzo, riso, melone, or rosemarina, or other tiny, seed-shaped pasta
Salt and freshly ground black pepper
2 tablespoons chopped radish leaves
3 slices Preserved Lemons (page 196), finely slivered, plus 4 slices for garnish
1 tablespoon red wine vinegar, medium acid

Place the chicken breasts in a large, nonreactive dish. Whisk together the garlic, lemon juice, and mustard oil and spoon about half the mixture over the chicken. Set the remainder of the dressing aside. Cover and refrigerate the chicken, turning the breasts every hour or so for 3 to 4 hours. Trim the radishes (save the leaves), slice them $\frac{1}{8}$-inch thick, and hold them in ice water until ready to use.

Before finishing the dish, let the chicken rest at room temperature for 30 minutes. Cook the pasta according to package directions. Drain and rinse it, toss with 1 tablespoon of the dressing, and keep warm.

Drain the marinade from the chicken into a heavy skillet and set it aside. Season the chicken breasts with salt and pepper. Place them in the skillet and cook them, covered, over medium heat for about 8 to 10 minutes, turning them every 2 or 3 minutes.

Drain the radishes and just before the chicken is done, sauté them in a small amount of the dressing for about 2 minutes, until they turn bright red. Season with salt, a few turns of pepper, and the red wine vinegar.

Add the chopped radish leaves and slivered preserved lemons to the reserved dressing and season with salt and pepper. Divide the pasta among 4 individual serving plates. Place a portion of chicken on each plate, draping it partially over the pasta. Add the sautéed radishes and spoon the dressing over each serving. Garnish each plate with a slice of preserved lemon, a single radish, and a couple of turns of black pepper. Serve immediately.

Sautéed Chicken Dijon

The dish comes from mustard's heartland, Dijon itself. Its preparation is featured in the Spice of Life *film on mustard, and although a specific recipe is not given, I believe this version captures the spirit if not the letter of the recipe named in honor of Madame Gaston Gerard, wife of a former mayor of Dijon. The inclusion of cheese in the sauce is said to be her inspiration; the whole cloves of garlic are my contribution. Serve with steamed rice or roasted new potatoes.*

1 roasting chicken, 4 to 5 pounds	3 to 4 tablespoons Dijon mustard
Salt and freshly ground black pepper	5 ounces Gruyère cheese, grated
1 tablespoon butter	4 tablespoons fresh Italian parsley, minced
1 tablespoon olive oil	1 cup Mustard Bread Crumbs (page 193)
5 or 6 cloves garlic	
½ cup dry white wine	
2 cups heavy cream	

Cut the chicken into pieces (thigh, leg, single breast, wing), rinse, pat dry, and season with salt and pepper. Melt the butter with the olive oil in a large, heavy skillet over medium heat and sauté the whole cloves of garlic, turning often so that they do not burn. When they begin to soften, remove from the pan and set aside. Place the chicken parts in the pan and sauté until golden brown on each side. Transfer to a small baking dish and place in a 325°F oven for about 20 minutes.

Pour off any extra fat in the skillet. Deglaze the pan with the wine over medium heat. Return the garlic to the pan and reduce the wine until there is just a bit left. Using a fork, mash the garlic, which should be soft by this time, add the cream, and reduce by one third. Stir in the mustard, half the cheese, and half the parsley.

Pull the chicken from the oven, pour the sauce over it, and top with the remaining cheese, the parsley, and the bread crumbs. Place under a preheated broiler until the cheese melts and the top is golden. Serve immediately.

Chicken Stuffed Under the Skin, Two Ways

Serves 4

Good poultry stuffing is all too often relegated to the holidays. These two versions feature it in smaller portions, making it possible to enjoy the fragrant mix of bread and juices without having to cook a large meal. The first version, using Dijon mustard, is rich and savory; the second version, with honey and candied citrus peel, joins the sweetness of honey with the sharpness of mustard in an always pleasing combination. Serve the chicken atop steamed rice.

DIJON STUFFING:

3 tablespoons butter
1 small yellow onion, diced
2 celery stalks, minced
1 teaspoon fresh thyme leaves, plus sprigs for garnish
½ teaspoon minced fresh summer savory, plus sprigs for garnish
4 tablespoons extra-forte Dijon mustard
1 teaspoon freshly ground black pepper
3 cups fresh sourdough bread crumbs
4 chicken breasts, 6 to 8 ounces each (see Note)
2 cups homemade chicken stock

Melt the butter in a heavy skillet over medium heat and sauté the onion until soft. Add the celery and continue to sauté the mixture until the celery is soft and the onion transparent. Remove the mixture from the heat, add the thyme, savory, and two tablespoons of the mustard. Toss this mixture with the pepper, the bread crumbs, and just enough of the chicken stock to barely moisten the stuffing.

Preheat an oven to 400°F. Loosen the skin of each chicken breast, being careful not to detach the skin completely. Slip the stuffing between the skin and the flesh of each breast. Set the breasts on a rack in a roasting pan and place in the oven. Bake until the breasts are done but still tender, about 35 to 45 minutes.

Add a thyme and a savory sprig to the remaining chicken stock and reduce it by two thirds at high heat. Remove from the heat, discard the herbs, and stir in the remaining 2 tablespoons of mustard. About 5 minutes before the chicken finishes cooking, brush it with the sauce and add a turn or two of freshly milled black pepper.

Remove the chicken from the oven and let it rest for 5 minutes. To serve, top the chicken with the Dijon sauce and garnish with the remaining sprigs of herbs.

Note: Your cooking time will vary a great deal depending on the size of the breasts.

HONEY & CITRUS STUFFING:

- ½ cup Zante currants
- 2 cups homemade chicken stock
- 3 tablespoons butter
- 1 small yellow onion, diced
- 2 celery stalks, minced
- ¼ cup candied lemon peel
- ¼ cup candied orange peel
- 3 cups fresh sourdough bread crumbs
- ½ cup Honey-Pepper Mustard (page 174) or Honey-Ginger Mustard (page 175)
- 1 teaspoon freshly ground black pepper
- 4 chicken breasts, 6 to 8 ounces each (see Note, above)

To make the honey stuffing, soak the currants in enough of the chicken stock to cover for 1 hour. Strain the currants, reserving the stock. Melt the butter in a heavy skillet over medium heat and sauté the onion until soft. Add the celery and continue to sauté the mixture until the celery is soft and the onion transparent. Remove the mixture from the heat, add the currants, lemon peel, orange peel, three tablespoons of the mustard, and the pepper. Toss this mixture with the bread crumbs and just enough of the chicken stock to barely moisten the stuffing.

Preheat the oven to 400°F. Loosen the skin of each chicken breast, being careful not to detach the skin completely. Slip the stuffing between the skin and the flesh of each breast. Set the breasts on a rack in a roasting pan and place in the oven. Bake until the breasts are done, but still tender, about 35 to 45 minutes.

Combine the reserved chicken stock with the remaining chicken stock and reduce it by two thirds at high heat. Remove the reduced stock from the heat and add the remaining mustard. About 5 minutes before the chicken finishes cooking, brush it with the sauce.

Remove the chicken from the oven and let it rest for 5 minutes. To serve, top the chicken with the mustard sauce.

Chicken Baked with Mustard

Serves 4

This dish can also be made using duck legs, although they are generally harder to come by than chicken legs. They take longer to cook, too, so adjust the time accordingly and allow about an hour.

½ cup Dijon mustard
3 cloves garlic, pressed, plus 2 cloves garlic, minced
2 teaspoons soy sauce
1 teaspoon dried thyme leaves, crushed

3 tablespoons olive oil
4 full chicken legs (thigh and leg connected), 4 chicken breast halves, or 4 full duck legs
1 cup Mustard Bread Crumbs (page 193)

Whisk together the mustard, both pressed and minced garlic, soy sauce, thyme, and olive oil. Coat each chicken or duck piece with the mustard mixture and roll it in the bread crumbs. Place the meat on a rack in a roasting pan and bake in a 375°F oven until done, about 30 to 40 minutes for chicken and longer for duck, depending on the poultry part and its size. Remove from the oven and serve immediately.

Roast Duckling with Cranberry-Mustard Sauce

Serves 2 or 3

The rich dark meat of duck pairs beautifully with the deeper-flavored fruits like plums, blueberries, blackberries, and cranberries. In this version of that classic marriage, I enjoy the flash of tartness contributed by the cranberries, and accent the flavor by serving either Cranberry-Rhubarb Sauce (page 189) or Rhubarb-Strawberry Chutney with Mustard Seeds (page 193) on the side. The Spicy Glazed Carrots on page 137 make an ideal accompaniment.

1 duckling, about 5 pounds
Salt and freshly ground black pepper
1 yellow onion, cut in half
1 orange stuck with 8 whole cloves
2 cups (about 6 ounces) fresh cranberries

2 to 6 tablespoons sugar
2 cups duck or veal stock
1 teaspoon very finely minced orange zest
1 to 2 tablespoons Dijon mustard
2 teaspoons butter

Rinse the duck and pat dry. Season the cavity with the salt and pepper and place the onion and the orange inside. Prick the skin of the duck all over to allow the fat to run off during roasting. Place the duck on a rack in a roasting pan and bake at 400°F until tender, about 45 minutes.

While the duck is cooking, place the cranberries in a small, heavy saucepan with 2 tablespoons of the sugar. Simmer over very low heat until they are quite soft. Purée with an immersion blender or in a food processor and press through a sieve or food mill. Set aside.

When the duck is done, remove it from the oven and place it on a warmed platter. Keep warm until ready to serve. Over medium heat on the stove top, deglaze the pan with some of the duck stock. Add the rest of the stock to the pan and reduce the mixture by about one third. Stir in the puréed cranberries, the orange zest, the mustard, and enough of the remaining sugar to balance the sauce. Taste the sauce again, and correct the balance with salt and pepper. Finish the sauce by whisking in the butter a teaspoon at a time. Remove the sauce from the heat, carve the duck, and serve immediately with the sauce on the side.

Grilled Rib-Eye Steak with Fennel, Red Onions, Cucumbers, & Horseradish-Mustard Sauce

Serves 4 as a main course, or 8 as a first course

The best part of this dish is the way the juices of the meat mingle with the flavors of horseradish, mustard, and lemon. The bright crispness of the vegetables forms a very pleasant contrasting texture as well. This dish is perfect for beef lovers who want to cut down on their consumption of red meat. Although the overall dish is substantial and pleasantly filling, the beef is limited to about four ounces per serving, half that if you serve it as a first course.

1 large or two small fennel bulbs, very thinly sliced

1 red onion, very thinly sliced

1 cucumber, peeled and thinly sliced

2 boneless rib-eye or market steaks, about ½ pound each

Salt and freshly ground black pepper

1 tablespoon extra virgin olive oil

Juice of ½ lemon

½ cup sour cream

2 to 3 tablespoons Dijon mustard

1 to 2 tablespoons prepared creamy horseradish

2 tablespoons half-and-half

Japanese red mustard or other crisp greens

Combine the fennel, onion, and cucumber and toss well. Cover and chill until ready to serve.

Prepare a charcoal fire or preheat a broiler. Grill or broil the steaks until rare or medium-rare, depending on preference. Season with salt and pepper and let rest for 3 to 4 minutes.

Add the olive oil and lemon juice to the vegetables and toss. Arrange a small mound of them on each of 4 plates (or 8 plates if serving as a first course). Quickly mix together the sour cream, mustard, horseradish, and half-and-half and transfer to a squeeze bottle. Slice the steaks thinly against the grain and divide them among the plates, placing the slices atop the vegetables. Top each portion with about 1 tablespoon of the horseradish-mustard sauce and garnish with a spoonful of the sauce on the side, along with a handful of the Japanese red mustard. Serve immediately.

Honey-Mustard Marinated Steak with Basmati Rice

Serves 4

In a mustard cookbook, it would be unthinkable not to offer several beef recipes, mustard and beef having been happy companions since early history. But today's diet includes less red meat than it once did and many people are giving it up entirely. Health and environmental considerations are, of course, essential, but I opt for a varied diet with an eye to health that includes everything I love but with limited amounts of undeniably delicious-but-bad-for-you saturated fats. Better than a huge steak, these slices of rare grilled beef are sensational with the sweet heat of the honey-mustard dressing.

1 cup All-Purpose Mustard Sauce (page 188)

⅓ cup Honey-Ginger Mustard (page 175)

2 rib-eye or market steaks, 8 to 12 ounces each

1 cup basmati rice

2 tablespoons pure olive oil

2 tablespoons finely minced red onion

2 teaspoons yellow mustard seeds

¼ cup Zante currants

2 tablespoons diced candied lemon peel

2 tablespoons candied orange peel

Salt and freshly ground black pepper

Four fresh mint sprigs

Mix together the mustard sauce and Honey-Ginger Mustard. Coat the steaks with a generous amount of the mixture and let them rest in a nonreactive container for at least two hours in the refrigerator. Reserve the remaining sauce. Thirty minutes before serving, cook the rice according to package directions. Preheat a charcoal grill or a broiler.

Heat the olive oil in a sauté pan over medium heat and sauté the onions until soft. Add the mustard seeds and sauté for 2 minutes. Add the currants, lemon peel, and orange peel and toss the ingredients together to heat through. Remove from the heat and add 3 tablespoons of the reserved sauce. Toss the ingredients with the cooked rice and set aside; keep the mixture warm.

Brush most of the marinade off the steaks and grill or broil them until rare or medium-rare. Remove from the heat, season with salt and pepper and let rest 3 or 4 minutes. Slice the steaks thinly against the grain. Divide the rice among 4 serving plates and top each portion with sliced steak. Top each serving with a spoonful of the remaining sauce, garnish with a sprig of mint, and serve immediately.

Beef Tenderloin with Mustard Butter & Roasted Shallot & Red Wine Sauce

Serves 6 to 8

Although mustard, plain and unadorned, is a wonderful—perhaps the ideal—condiment for beef, special occasions sometimes call for a more elegant dish with more complex preparation. A finely honed sauce served with a well-cooked beef tenderloin is the perfect dish for such an occasion. In this version, the mustard plays a more subtle role than it generally does used as a condiment. Serve the tenderloin with roasted new potatoes.

1 beef tenderloin (head fillet), about 3 pounds
Salt and freshly ground black pepper
4 large shallots, unpeeled
Pure olive oil
6 cups beef, veal, or duck stock
2 cups full-bodied red wine such as Zinfandel or Cabernet Sauvignon

Bouquet garni of fresh oregano, thyme, and Italian parsley sprigs
1 tablespoon Dijon mustard
1 tablespoon butter
½ cup Mustard Butter (page 185)
6 to 8 fresh Italian parsley sprigs

Trim the tenderloin, removing the silver skin and any excess fat and saving all bits of meat that you cut off. Season the tenderloin with salt and pepper. You can prepare the tenderloin in advance, but be sure to remove it from the refrigerator 30 minutes before cooking time.

Rub the shallots generously with the olive oil, place in a baking dish, put in a 325°F oven, and roast them until tender, about 40 minutes. Remove the shallots from the oven and let cool. When they are cool enough to handle, remove the skins and purée the soft interiors in a blender or food processor, adding a little of the stock if necessary to achieve smoothness. Set the purée aside.

Increase the oven temperature to 450°F. Brown the beef trimmings (you'll need about ¼ pound) over high heat in a heavy skillet with a little olive oil. When the meat is well browned on all sides, add ½ cup of the stock, deglaze the pan, and simmer until the stock is reduced to a glaze. Repeat, using ½ cup stock at a time, until you have used 4 cups. Do not reduce the final addition of stock all the way to a glaze, but only by half. Strain the essence into a heavy saucepan and set aside.

Place the red wine and bouquet garni in a heavy saucepan over medium heat and reduce by three fourths, until about ½ cup remains. Strain the reduced wine into the stock essence. Put the beef tenderloin on a rack in a roasting pan and roast in the preheated oven. After 10 minutes, reduce the heat to 375°F and cook the tenderloin approximately 25 minutes, or until it reaches an internal temperature of 125°F for rare beef. Cook an additional 10 to 15 minutes, or to an internal temperature of 140°F for medium-rare. Remove the tenderloin from the oven and let rest for 5 minutes.

To complete the sauce, stir 2 tablespoons of the puréed shallots into the wine-stock essence mixture. Add the remaining 2 cups stock and reduce the mixture by one third. Add the Dijon mustard and salt and pepper to taste. Taste the mixture again, adding more roasted shallot purée, more mustard, and additional salt and pepper to balance the sauce. Finish the sauce by whisking in the butter.

To serve the tenderloin, slice it thinly against the grain. Place a ladleful of sauce on warmed individual plates and arrange the beef slices on top of the sauce. Top each serving with a small round of Mustard Butter and a sprig of Italian parsley.

Beef Tongue in Mustard Vinegar Sauce with Roasted Garlic & Saffron-Mustard Cream

Serves 6

Although no longer as popular as it once was, beef tongue has an extraordinarily good flavor. It is unfortunate that its culinary possibilities are so frequently overlooked. This recipe is based on a traditional French dish, with a few special touches added. The roasted garlic purée adds a creamy depth of flavor, with the Saffron-Mustard Cream acting as a bright counterpoint to it.

1 beef tongue, 4 to 5 pounds
1 quart homemade beef stock or 1 can (16 ounces) beef broth diluted with enough water to make 1 quart
1½ cups red wine vinegar (medium acid)
3 tablespoons roasted garlic purée (see Note, page 142)
⅓ cup Dijon mustard
Salt and freshly ground black pepper
Saffron Mustard Cream (page 187)

To poach the tongue, place it in a large stock pot and add the beef stock, ¾ cup of the vinegar, and enough water to completely cover it. Simmer, uncovered, over low heat until the meat is very tender, about 1½ to 2 hours. Remove from the heat and let the tongue cool in the liquid. When the liquid is at room temperature, remove the tongue and reduce the liquid to 2 cups.

Peel the skin from the tongue, cutting away any skin that remains, and remove any bones at the root end. Slice the tongue diagonally into slices ¼ inch thick. Arrange the slices in an ovenproof dish. Add the remaining ¾ cup vinegar to the reduced liquid and reduce it again to 2 cups. Stir the roasted garlic purée and the mustard into the reduced sauce, and add salt and pepper to taste. Pour the sauce over the tongue, cover, and bake it in a 350°F oven for 20 minutes.

Remove the tongue from the oven and let it rest 5 minutes. Serve it hot with the Saffron Mustard Cream alongside.

Grilled Sausages & Onions with Assorted Mustards

Serves 8

There are times when nothing hits the spot quite like some great sausages and beer. During the dog days of August, they're perfect cooked over an outdoor grill as the sun sinks and there is a bit of relief from the heat of the day.

2 pounds small onions, preferably torpedo
Pure olive oil
3 pounds assorted sausages such as Cajun, hot-beer, and German
Crusty french rolls, split, or good crusty bread
Dijon mustard
Coarse-grain mustard
All-Purpose Mustard Sauce (page 188)

The Devil's Mustard (page 173) or Roasted-Garlic Mustard (page 181)
Honey-Pepper Mustard (page 174)
Plum-Mustard Sauce (page 190)
Summer Potato Salad with Radishes & Green Beans (page 155) or Creamy Potato Salad with Eggs (see variation, page 147)

Prepare coals for grilling and begin once they have settled down to a moderate glow. Trim the onions; if they are very big, cut them in half. Rub the onions with the olive oil and place them on the grill. When the first side begins to brown, turn them and add the sausages to the grill. After about 5 minutes, turn the sausages. Most sausages (about 1 to 1¼ inches in diameter) will take 15 to 20 minutes to cook through. The onions, unless they are very small, will take about the same amount of time. Remove the sausages and onions to a large platter.

If you want, quickly grill the rolls or bread and place on the table with the sausages and onions. Have the various mustards and mustard sauces ready, along with the potato salad. Let guests assemble their plates as they want. Some may want to slather one of the mustards on a roll and top it with a sausage and slice of grilled onion. Others may want to put some of each mustard and sauce on a plate and eat the sausages in slices, dipping them into the different condiments. Be sure to serve plenty of cold beer.

Bockwurst Sandwiches with Onion-Mustard Sauce

Serves 4

This is German pub food at its best. When I had a small restaurant in Sonoma County, I served these sandwiches during an Oktoberfest celebration. We couldn't keep up with the demand, and I spent the day making batch after batch of onion sauce, finally selling nearly two hundred of the white veal and pork sausages to hungry revelers.

2 tablespoons pure olive oil
1 pound white or yellow onions, thinly sliced
1 cup beef stock

2 to 4 tablespoons mustard such as Dijon, German coarse-grain, or English coarse-grain

Salt and freshly ground	4 sourdough French rolls,
black pepper	split
4 bockwurst	

Prepare a charcoal fire or preheat a broiler. In a skillet heat the olive oil over medium heat. Add the onions and sauté until they are very limp and transparent, about 15 minutes. Add the beef stock and simmer for 5 minutes. Stir in the mustard and season to taste with salt and pepper. Set aside.

Grill or broil the sausages, for about 15 minutes, turning to brown all sides. Toast the French rolls. Place a sausage in each roll and top with a generous portion of the onion mixture. Serve with cold beer.

Pork Loin with Apricot-Mustard Glaze

Serves 4

Pork and apricots are one of the great culinary marriages. In this simple but elegant version, the mustard adds another dimension. Grilled or braised fennel or sautéed zucchini would make excellent side dishes. During apricot season, grill or bake apricots to serve alongside the pork.

½ cup apricot jam

3 tablespoons Dijon
mustard or coarse-grain
mustard

1 cup white wine (prefer-
ably a slightly sweet
wine like Gewurtztra-
miner, although a dry
white wine will do)

1 pork tenderloin, about
1½ pounds

1 pound apricots, in season

Salt and freshly ground
black pepper

Mix together the apricot jam, mustard, and about ¼ cup of
the wine, so that the mixture is fairly thick but easily spread-
able. Place the pork in a glass or ceramic dish, pour the mixture over it, cover, and refrigerate for 2 or 3 hours, turning
the pork every ½ hour or so. Remove from the refrigerator
30 minutes before cooking. Place the tenderloin on a rack in

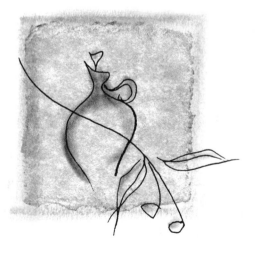

a small roasting pan and roast in a 350°F oven until it reaches an internal temperature of 160°F, about 20 minutes.

Meanwhile, if they are available, cut the apricots in half lengthwise and remove the stones. Brush the apricots with a bit of the marinade and bake them in a small pan alongside the pork for about 15 minutes, or grill them over low coals for 5 minutes, beginning when you remove the roast from the oven.

Remove the pork from the oven and let it rest for 5 minutes. On the stove top, deglaze the roasting pan with the remaining ¾ cup wine. Add the rest of the marinade and simmer until the liquid is reduced by half. Taste the sauce and season with salt and pepper.

Cut the pork into slices ⅛ inch thick and arrange on 4 serving plates. Divide the apricot halves among the plates and spoon plenty of sauce over the pork. Serve immediately.

Pork Loin in a Mustard Crust with Orange-Mustard Sauce

Serves 6 to 8

Instead of using the tenderloin of the pork, this recipe uses the entire loin, making it a good dish for a larger group. Most of the work can be completed ahead of time, which adds to the appeal of this entrée as the centerpiece of a dinner party.

1 boneless pork loin, 4 to
   5 pounds

DRY MARINADE:

2 tablespoons grated or-
   ange zest
4 cloves garlic, minced

1 tablespoon coarsely
   ground black pepper
1 teaspoon kosher salt

MUSTARD COATING:

4 cloves garlic, minced
¼ cup chopped green on-
   ions
1 cup Dijon mustard
½ cup fresh orange juice
   (from blood oranges, if
   available)

1 teaspoon freshly ground
   black pepper
1 teaspoon kosher salt
½ cup snipped fresh chives
2 tablespoons white mus-
   tard seeds

SAUCE:

1½ cups orange juice
   (from blood oranges, if
   available)
2 cups veal or duck stock
2 tablespoons Dijon mus-
   tard

1 teaspoon grated orange
   zest
1 tablespoon snipped
   chives
Salt and freshly ground
   black pepper

The night before cooking, trim any excess fat from the pork
loin. Combine the ingredients for the dry marinade and rub
it into the loin. Place the pork in a glass or ceramic dish,
cover, and refrigerate.

   Thirty minutes before you want to cook the loin, remove it from the refrigerator. To make the coating, combine
the garlic, green onions, mustard, orange juice, pepper, and

salt. Toss together the chives and mustard seeds. Have a roasting pan and rack ready, with the oven heated to 400°F. Spread the coating over the entire surface of the pork and then sprinkle the chive mixture over it. Place the loin on the rack and put it in the oven. Bake about 30 to 40 minutes, until it reaches an internal temperature of 160°F. Remove from the oven and let rest while you make the sauce.

To make the sauce, in a heavy saucepan combine the orange juice and stock, and reduce the mixture by half. Stir in the mustard, orange zest, and chives, taste the sauce, and add salt and pepper as needed. Keep the sauce warm while you cut the pork into thin slices. Arrange the slices on a platter and spoon some of the sauce over them. Serve immediately, with the remaining sauce in a bowl on the side.

Baby Back Ribs

Serves 4

These ribs are tender, just slightly sweet, and full of the subtle aroma of the ginger, garlic, and mustard. This is a very well-balanced marinade, in which each ingredient plays a crucial role but none dominates. In testing this recipe, I found that the longer the ribs marinated, the more delicate was the flavor, so give them as much time as you can. These ribs are delicious on their own, but certainly serve additional sweet coarse-grain mustard on the side if you wish. Accompany with coleslaw, potato salad, or steamed jasmine rice.

MARINADE:

½ cup coarse-grain mustard

½ cup firmly packed brown sugar

3 tablespoons minced garlic

3 tablespoons grated fresh ginger

3 shallots, minced

½ cup rice vinegar

1 cup soy sauce

4 to 5 pounds baby back ribs, in slabs

Stir together all the ingredients for the marinade. Rub each slab of ribs with the marinade, place them in a shallow pan, and pour the rest of the marinade over them. Cover and marinate the ribs for at least 24 hours or for up to 72 hours. Prepare a charcoal fire. Grill over hot coals, turning once, or bake on a rack in a 400°F oven until done, about 20 minutes. Serve immediately.

VARIATIONS:

1. Use chicken drummettes (the meaty part of the wing) instead of ribs. Marinate the chicken for 24 hours. Place the drummettes in a baking dish (do not crowd them) and bake at 325°F for 40 minutes.

2. Marinate slices or cubes of pork for 24 hours, thread on skewers with wedges of onion and fresh pineapple, and grill or broil. Serve with jasmine rice and a spicy mustard sauce for dipping.

Lamb in Mustard Marinade

Serves 4

I like to serve this lamb with plenty of rice alongside to soak up the delicious juices.

MARINADE:
1/4 cup honey, warmed
1/4 cup sherry
1/4 cup Dijon mustard

2 tablespoons minced
fresh rosemary
1 tablespoon freshly
ground black pepper

2 lamb loins, about 1 1/4
pounds each; 8 loin
lamb chops; or 2
pounds of lamb meat,
cut into 2-inch cubes

Fresh rosemary sprigs

Mix together the honey, sherry, mustard, rosemary, and pepper. Pour the marinade over the lamb, making sure that it coats the meat completely. Refrigerate for up to 48 hours before cooking.

Remove from the refrigerator 30 minutes before cooking. Place tenderloins or chops on a roasting rack and bake or broil until they are just done, about 12 minutes in a 375°F oven or 6 minutes on each side under the broiler. If using cubed lamb, thread the pieces on metal or bamboo skewers (bamboo skewers should be first soaked in water for

1 hour) and broil, turning once, for 7 minutes. Serve immediately, garnished with sprigs of rosemary.

Oven-Roasted Leg of Lamb with Sausage Stuffing & Mustard Glaze

Serves 6 to 8

This is the first recipe I ever published, long ago in a column entitled, "Try Lamb for Easter." It appears here with very few alterations, and is as delicious now as it was then, festive and perfect for a special occasion. In choosing the lamb you will use, try to find young American lamb, which has a much better flavor than either older American or imported lamb. Here in Sonoma County, Bellweather Farms and C. K. Lamb both produce outstanding lamb that is fed on local grasses and harvested before a fattening process that much commercial lamb goes through. The process adds weight—fat—to the animals, and inferior commercial feed is used.

1 leg of lamb, boned and butterflied, about 5 pounds
Pure olive oil
1 small yellow onion, chopped
8 cloves garlic, minced

1 pound Italian sausage, removed from the casings
2 tablespoons Dijon mustard
1 teaspoon fresh thyme leaves
1 teaspoon fresh summer savory leaves

1 teaspoon minced fresh
rosemary

1 cup fresh bread crumbs
1 tablespoon butter

MUSTARD GLAZE:
¾ cup Dijon mustard
½ cup pure olive oil
1 teaspoon soy sauce
1 teaspoon fresh thyme
leaves
1 teaspoon fresh summer
savory leaves

1 teaspoon minced fresh
rosemary
1 teaspoon freshly ground
black pepper
3 cloves garlic, pressed

½ cup water or stock

1 tablespoon butter,
chilled, cut into bits

Remove the papery outer covering of the lamb (the fell),
the silver skin, and any large strips of fat. Set the meat aside.
Heat a small amount of the olive oil in a heavy skillet over
medium heat and sauté the onions until soft and transparent. Add the garlic and sauté for another 2 minutes. Add the
sausage, crumble it with a fork, and cook until it is about
half-done. Stir in the mustard and fresh herbs. Add the
bread crumbs and toss. Remove the mixture from the heat
and set aside briefly.

Make the glaze by whisking all the ingredients together until smooth.

Place the boned leg of lamb, outside down, on a flat
working surface. Brush some of the glaze over inside surface, and then spread the stuffing over it. Roll up the leg
and tie it. Place on a rack in a roasting pan. Cover the outer
surface of the lamb with the glaze, place it in a 325°F oven,

and bake for 20 minutes per pound for a medium-rare roast, or until it reaches an internal temperature of between 130 and 135°F. Remove the lamb from the oven and let it rest for 15 minutes before slicing. Place the roasting pan on the stove top over low heat. Add the water or stock and deglaze the pan. Add any leftover mustard glaze, stir well, and simmer for about 5 minutes. Add the butter, a piece at a time, stirring after each addition until the butter is just melted. Pour the sauce into a warmed bowl.

Cut the lamb into slices ¼ inch thick and arrange on a platter. Top with some of the sauce. Pass the remaining sauce on the side.

VARIATION:

The mustard glaze is also excellent with baked ham. Simply spread half the glaze on the ham and bake according to the size and type of ham. When it is nearly done, spread the remaining glaze over the ham. When the ham is done, let it rest for 15 minutes before slicing. Serve with mustard or additional mustard glaze on the side.

French Sausage Loaf with Mustard

Serves 6

I make several versions of this stuffed French bread, and find it a very handy technique for feeding a large group of people. The loaves can be stuffed in advance, but to serve them hot, be sure to allow extra time at a lower temperature if you begin with a chilled loaf. This is also an excel-

*lent picnic item; keep it chilled until ready to slice and eat. And don't for-
get to take along plenty of additional Dijon mustard.*

1 large, fat loaf San Francisco–style sourdough
bread
1 small yellow onion, diced
Pure olive oil
1 pound bulk pork sau-
sage or ground lamb
2 tablespoons minced garlic
1 egg
3 tablespoons plus 2 tea-
spoons Dijon mustard

2 tablespoons finely
minced fresh Italian
parsley
1 teaspoon finely minced
fresh rosemary (if using
lamb)
Salt and freshly ground
black pepper
2 tablespoons butter

Cut the ends off the loaf of bread and, with your fingers,
pull out the soft insides of the bread, making a shell. Using
a food processor, make bread crumbs from the inside of the
loaf and set them aside, along with the ends of the loaf.

Sauté the onion in a little olive oil until soft and transparent. Add the sausage or lamb and sauté it with the onions, using a fork to keep it crumbly. When it is nearly
done, add the garlic and sauté for another 2 minutes. Remove from the heat and cool slightly.

Mix together the egg, 3 tablespoons of the mustard,
and the parsley (and the rosemary, if using) and add it to the
meat mixture, along with the bread crumbs. Toss the mixture together quickly and lightly. Season with salt and pepper and let cool until it is easy to handle.

Fill the inside of the hollowed loaf of bread with the
sausage mixture, packing it in fairly tightly. Place the ends

on the loaf and, if necessary, hold them in place with toothpicks. Melt the butter in a saucepan, remove it from the heat, stir in the remaining mustard, and brush the surface of the loaf with the butter. Wrap the loaf in aluminum foil and bake in a 375°F oven for about 20 minutes.

Let the loaf rest for 5 minutes before serving in thick, 1½-inch slices, with plenty of Dijon mustard on the side. This loaf is also delicious served at room temperature.

Ham with Red-Eye Gravy

Serves 10 to 12

I have been intrigued by the thought of combining coffee and mustard since I read M. F. K. Fisher's comment about Frederick the Great's habit of doing so. He made his coffee with Champagne instead of water, she tells us in Serve It Forth, *and then stirred in powdered mustard to make the flavors stronger. "Now to me it seems improbable that Frederick truly liked this brew," Fisher comments. "I suspect him of bravado. Or perhaps he was taste-blind." I agreed, and then I came across a recipe for ham with red-eye gravy that combined both coffee and mustard in substantial quantities. I don't think I'd want to drink a cup of the stuff first thing in the morning, but for a hearty dinner, it is quite good.*

The best dry-cured, country hams require long soaking and simmering, but the results are well worth the effort.

1 cured ham, 10 to 12 pounds	**water to cover**
	2 yellow onions, quartered

1 head of garlic, cut in half

3 cups apple cider vinegar, medium acid

3 cups strongly brewed black coffee

1 cup brown sugar, firmly packed

1 cup mustard, either prepared brown or Dijon, extra-forte

Soak the ham in cold water for 24 hours. Drain the ham and scrub it to remove any mold that might be present. In a large kettle or stock pot, simmer the ham with the onions and garlic in enough water to cover it for 15 minutes per pound. Add the apple cider vinegar to the water for the last hour of cooking. In a small saucepan, mix together the coffee, brown sugar, and mustard. Heat the mixture, stirring, until the sugar dissolves.

Transfer the ham from the kettle to the rack of a roasting pan and carefully remove the skin and trim the fat, leaving just $1/4$ inch of fat on the ham. Brush the ham with the coffee glaze, and place it in an oven preheated to 400°F. Baste the ham with additional glaze every 15 minutes and bake the ham for about 1 hour until it reaches an internal temperature of 160°F. Remove the ham from the oven, transfer to a platter, and place the roasting pan over medium heat. Add the remaining coffee glaze to the roasting pan, deglaze the pan, scraping up any particles, and reduce the glaze by about one half, until it is the consistency of a thin syrup. Carve the ham, slicing it very thinly, and serve it immediately with the sauce on the side.

Céleri Rémoulade

Serves 4 to 6

Celery root is a wonderful vegetable, and one that has never been very popular in this country. It is, however, a traditional bistro dish in France, where it is prepared much as I recommend here. Although not traditional, céleri rémoulade is outstanding served with gravlax and croutons and very good served alongside golden beets tossed with just a little olive oil.

1 cup crème fraîche (see Note)
¼ cup imported Dijon mustard
1 to 2 tablespoons fresh lemon juice (optional)

Salt and freshly ground black pepper
1 celery root, about 1¼ pounds

Mix together the *crème fraîche* and mustard. Taste and if you prefer a bit of tartness, add the lemon juice. Season with salt and pepper and set aside.

Peel the celery root, cutting away any green and all the brown skin. Quarter the root and grate in a food processor.

Place the grated celery root in a large mixing bowl and toss with the dressing until it is well coated. Serve as a first course or as a side dish.

VARIATION:

Serve *Céleri Rémoulade* with Gravlax with Mustard Cream (page 63). Divide the celery root among 4 to 6 serving plates and drape 4 slices of the gravlax halfway across each serving. Garnish with a small spoonful of the Mustard Cream and a sprig of fresh rosemary.

Note: Substitute the following if *crème fraîche* is unavailable: Mix ⅔ cup sour cream with ⅓ cup heavy cream. Cover and let sit unrefrigerated for about 6 hours or overnight.

Spicy Glazed Carrots

Serves 6

If you have access to a good farm market, by all means try to find organic carrots. Properly grown, they are sweeter and much more delicious than most supermarket carrots. This is a simple dish, fairly sweet and quite good as a side dish with beef, pork, or chicken.

1 pound young, small
  carrots
2 tablespoons butter
2 tablespoons brown sugar
1 to 2 tablespoons Dijon
  or coarse-grain mustard

Salt and freshly ground
  black pepper
2 tablespoons chopped
  fresh Italian parsley

Trim the carrots and peel or scrape them. If they are *very* small, leave them whole. For larger carrots, cut them into medium julienne. Heat the butter and brown sugar in a heavy saucepan, add the carrots, cover, and cook until they are tender, 4 to 8 minutes, depending on the size of the carrots. Remove from the heat, stir in the mustard, season with salt and pepper, and place on a warmed serving plate. Sprinkle **the parsley over** the carrots and serve.

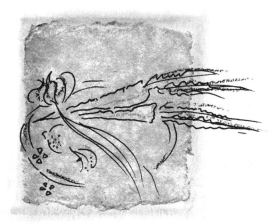

Julienned Carrots with Lemon-Mustard Dressing

Serves 6

These carrots are light and delicate, full of citrusy sweetness and crunch.

1 pound carrots, peeled and cut into small julienne
Juice of 2 lemons
2 tablespoons brown sugar
2 tablespoons coarse-grain mustard
1 teaspoon Dijon mustard
½ cup pure olive oil
Salt and freshly ground black pepper

Cook the carrots in rapidly boiling water until they are just tender. Rinse in cool water and drain. Mix together the lemon juice, sugar, and mustards. Whisk in the olive oil, taste, and season with salt and pepper.

Toss the carrots with the dressing and serve.

Oven-Roasted New Potatoes with Mustard-Chive Butter

Serves 4 to 6 as a side dish

Few things are better than perfect little chunks of roasted potatoes. This is simply another delicious variation on that theme.

2 pounds smallest new red
   potatoes, unpeeled
4 tablespoons butter
Freshly cracked black
   pepper

Mustard Butter (see vari-
   ations, page 186)
2 tablespoons snipped
   fresh chives
Salt

Scrub the potatoes and cook them in a large pot of rapidly boiling, salted water until they are about half done. They should still be fairly firm in the center. Drain, rinse, and dry the potatoes. This step of the recipe can be done well in advance.

Heat the butter in a heavy roasting pan or cast-iron skillet. Add the potatoes and black pepper and shake the pan to coat the potatoes in the butter and pepper. Place in a 325°F oven and roast until tender, about 30 minutes. Turn the potatoes twice during cooking.

Meanwhile, heat a serving bowl or dish and melt the Mustard Butter in it (do not place on direct heat, just in a warm spot). Remove the potatoes from the oven, lift them into the serving dish, and shake to coat them in the mustard butter. Add salt to taste, more pepper, and the chives. Serve immediately.

Mashed Potatoes with Roasted Garlic & Dijon Mustard

Serves 6

Serve this fragrant variation on a traditional favorite with flavors that will complement it and provide a pleasing contrast, rather than mirror the flavor of mustard. These potatoes would be excellent with meat loaf topped with puréed, sun-dried tomatoes, for example, or simple roast chicken. For a hearty winter meal, evocative of times past but spiced up for today's tastes, serve them with a grilled rib-eye steak. Simple steamed spinach or broccoli makes a perfect accompaniment. And, of course, a hearty red wine is a must. I don't recommend pairing them with main courses that feature mustard, such as ham with a mustard glaze or lamb in a mustard marinade. The unique depth of flavor provided by both the mustard and the roasted garlic should be allowed centerstage, without competition from similar tastes.

2 pounds mature potatoes
    (about 6)
⅓ cup half-and-half or
    milk
2 to 4 tablespoons butter

2 to 4 tablespoons roasted
    garlic purée (see Note)
2 tablespoons extra-forte
    Dijon mustard
Salt and freshly ground
    black pepper

Scrub the potatoes well and cut them into large chunks. For a smoother finished dish, peel them first. Cook in a large kettle of rapidly boiling, salted water until they are fork tender, about 20 minutes. Drain and let them rest, covered with a cloth towel, for 5 minutes.

Meanwhile, heat the half-and-half or milk and butter together until the butter has melted. Remove from the heat and stir in the garlic purée and mustard.

Mash the hot potatoes with a fork or potato masher or put them through a potato ricer. Beat the potatoes with the masher or fork with the butter mixture until the potatoes are light and fluffy. Serve immediately or hold, covered, over a *very* low flame for up to 10 minutes.

Note: To make roasted garlic purée, clean 2 or 3 heads of raw garlic, leaving the bulb intact but removing any dirt that may cling to the roots and as much of the dry outer skin as will come off easily. Place the bulbs in a small ovenproof dish or pan, add about ½ cup pure olive oil and ¼ cup water, season with salt and pepper, cover, and bake at 325°F for 45 to 60 minutes, until the garlic is the consistency of soft butter. Remove the garlic from the oven and let it cool on absorbent paper. When it is cool enough to be handled easily, set the garlic on a cutting board, remove the root, and use the heel of your hand to press out the garlic pulp. If necessary, squeeze the pulp out clove by clove. Scrape the garlic pulp off the cutting board, place it in a small bowl, and mash it with a fork until it is smooth. A head of garlic will yield approximately 2 tablespoons of purée.

# Gratin of Potatoes

Serves 6 to 8

On a cold winter's night few things are as satisfying as a deep dish of scalloped potatoes.

VERSION 1:

2 tablespoons butter
4 large waxy potatoes, peeled and sliced ⅛ inch thick
Salt and freshly ground black pepper
⅓ cup extra-forte Dijon mustard
1 ½ cups heavy cream
1 cup Mustard Bread Crumbs (page 193)

Butter the inside of a shallow, ovenproof baking dish. Layer the potatoes in the dish, adding salt and pepper to each layer. Mix together the mustard and the cream and pour it over the potatoes. Spread the bread crumbs over the surface and bake in a preheated 325°F oven until the cream has reduced and the potatoes are tender, about 40 minutes. Serve immediately.

VERSION 2:

1 clove garlic
2 tablespoons butter
2 sweet onions (preferably Walla Walla, Maui, or Vidalia), peeled and thinly sliced into rings
4 large waxy potatoes, peeled and sliced ⅛ inch thick
3 tablespoons snipped fresh chives
Salt and freshly ground black pepper

⅓ cup Dijon mustard
    flavored with green
    peppercorns

1½ cups homemade
    chicken stock or duck
    stock
1 cup Mustard Bread
    Crumbs (page 193)

With the side of a knife, crush the garlic and rub it all over the inside of a shallow, ovenproof baking dish, and then butter the dish. Layer the onions and potatoes alternately in the dish, adding a sprinkling of chives, salt, and pepper to each layer. Blend together the mustard and the stock, pour the mixture over the potatoes, and top with the bread crumbs. Cover the dish and bake in a 350°F oven for 30 minutes. Remove the cover and bake until the potatoes are tender and the top is nicely browned, about 15 minutes longer. Serve immediately.

Coleslaw with Ginger-Mustard Vinaigrette & Cilantro

Serves 6 to 8

Good coleslaw is hard to resist. Sweet or sour, crunchy or well marinated in its dressing, it is an all-time favorite with endless variations. This version is tart and sweet, and bright with the always enticing addition of cilantro.

1 small head red or green cabbage, shredded

3 or 4 carrots, peeled and grated

1 small red onion, diced

GINGER-MUSTARD VINAIGRETTE:

2 tablespoons apple cider vinegar

2 to 4 tablespoons fresh lemon juice

1 or 2 cloves garlic, pressed

2 teaspoons peeled and finely grated fresh ginger (or put through a garlic press)

2 teaspoons yellow mustard seeds

1 tablespoon sugar

2 tablespoons Dijon mustard

$\frac{2}{3}$ cup pure olive oil

3 tablespoons finely minced fresh cilantro leaves

Salt and freshly ground black pepper

145

Toss together all the vegetables. Make the dressing by whisking together the vinegar, lemon juice, garlic, ginger, sugar, and mustard. Slowly whisk in the oil and then add the cilantro. Taste the dressing and season with salt and pepper. Pour the vinaigrette over the vegetables and toss until well coated. Add the mustard seeds, toss again lightly, and serve immediately or cover and chill until ready to serve.

 ## Creamy Coleslaw

Serves 6 to 8

This version of one of America's favorite salads is seductively creamy. If you use Dijon mustard, you will have a smoother, slightly more subtle flavor than if you use a tart coarse-grain mustard. Both versions are delicious.

1 small head red or green cabbage, shredded
1 small red onion, diced
2 tablespoons red wine vinegar
1/4 cup pure olive oil
1/2 cup sour cream
1/2 cup good mayonnaise (homemade is best)

2 tablespoons Dijon mustard or coarse-grain mustard
Salt and freshly ground black pepper
3 tablespoons finely chopped fresh Italian parsley

Toss together the cabbage and onions. Make the dressing by whisking together the vinegar, olive oil, sour cream, mayonnaise, and mustard. Taste the dressing and season with salt and pepper. Pour the dressing over the vegetables. Add the parsley and toss together well. Serve immediately, or chill, covered, until ready to serve.

VARIATION:

CREAMY POTATO SALAD WITH EGGS: Omit the cabbage and onion. Combine 4 cups cooked and thinly sliced potatoes, peeled or not, with 1 bunch green onions, chopped; 2 sliced hard-boiled eggs, sliced; 1 teaspoon celery seeds; and all but 2 tablespoons of the dressing. Taste the salad and add salt and pepper. Place the salad on a serving plate and top it with 2 hard-boiled eggs, cut in halves or quarters. Spoon the remaining dressing over the eggs, add a few turns of black pepper, and serve.

Celery Root, Fennel, Apple, & Radish Salad

Serves 4 to 6

This salad is bright, crunchy, and refreshing, perfect as a light lunch on a hot day.

1 medium celery root, peeled

1 medium fennel bulb, trimmed

1 tart green apple, peeled and cored

1 bunch radishes, trimmed

Orange Mustard Cream (page 187)

Salt and freshly ground black pepper

2 bunches very fresh watercress, washed and trimmed, or several leaves of butter lettuce

Cut the celery root, fennel, apple, and radishes into matchstick-sized julienne. Hold in ice water until you are ready to dress the salad, up to 1 or 2 hours. If you have not already done so, make the mustard cream. Drain the vegetables and apple and toss them with the dressing. Taste the salad and season with salt and pepper. Arrange the watercress or lettuce leaves on individual serving plates and divide the salad among the plates. Add a few turns of pepper to each plate and serve.

Oranges, Onions, & Red Peppers with Mustard Greens

Serves 4 to 6

Here is a salad that offers a sensational interplay of flavors and textures, of savory and sweet, of creamy and crunchy, of cool and hot. I love it for lunch, with nothing but some good crusty bread alongside.

4 slices bacon
1 sweet onion (preferably Vidalia, Walla Walla, or Maui), slivered
1 sweet red pepper, slivered
3 oranges (preferably blood oranges), peeled, all white pith removed, sliced 1/4 inch thick

1 avocado, peeled and sliced lengthwise
1 quart young mustard greens
3 ounces young, fresh chèvre

ORANGE-MUSTARD VINAIGRETTE:

1/3 cup red wine vinegar	1 cup pure olive oil
Juice and grated zest of 1 orange	Salt and freshly ground black pepper
2 teaspoons Dijon mustard	

Sauté the bacon until just crisp and transfer it to absorbent paper. Make the vinaigrette by whisking together the vinegar, orange juice and zest, mustard, and olive oil. Season to taste with salt and pepper.

Toss together the onion, sweet pepper, and 3 tablespoons of the dressing. Set the mixture aside. Place the mustard greens on 1 large or 4 to 6 small serving plates. Arrange slices of oranges and avocadoes over the surface of the greens, and scatter the onion mixture over them. Drizzle with the remaining vinaigrette and crumble the goat cheese and the bacon on top. Serve immediately.

Pasta Flan Salad with Romaine Lettuce & Caesar-Style Dressing

Serves 6 as a main course lunch, or 12 as a first course

This is perhaps my favorite recipe in the book. It is as dramatic on the plate as it is delicious on the palate, a sort of dressed-up tribute to Caesar salad. I'm a dedicated lover of pasta, and I particularly enjoy the way you can sense the texture of the thin strands of angel hair in the larger context of the custard. It really is quite wonderful, and all of the fla-vors—anchovy, pancetta, *cheese, mustard—work together in happy harmony. This salad is filling, so accompaniments should be light. The custards can be made in advance, but should be removed from the refrig-erator at least 30 minutes before serving.*

¼ pound imported capel-lini (angel hair pasta) or spaghettini

Pure olive oil

3 ounces pancetta

4 eggs

2 cups milk

1 teaspoon hot mustard flour

3 teaspoons Dijon mustard

1 teaspoon freshly ground black pepper

6 ounces imported aged Asiago or parmigiano-reggiano cheese, grated on a medium blade

DRESSING:

1 egg yolk

Juice of 1 lemon, or more to taste

3 anchovy fillets

1 tablespoon Dijon mustard

3 cloves garlic

⅔ cup extra virgin olive oil

¼ cup freshly grated par-migiano-reggiano cheese

1 teaspoon freshly ground black pepper

Salt, if needed

6 large, thin slices day-old country-style french or Italian bread (or 12 if serving as a first course)

Pure olive oil

Salt and freshly ground black pepper

1 large or 2 small heads romaine lettuce

Cook the pasta according to package directions until it is *al-most* done, but still has a good bite at its core. While it is cooking, brush a 12-cup muffin pan lightly with olive oil. Sauté the *pancetta* until just crisp. Place it on absorbent paper, and when it is cool enough to handle, crumble or chop it very finely. Reserve 2 teaspoons of the *pancetta* and divide the rest among the muffin cups, placing it in the center of each. Beat the eggs and whisk in the milk, mustard flour, mustard, and black pepper.

Drain the pasta, rinse in cool water, and shake to remove as much water as possible. Toss it with a little olive oil (this will keep it easy to handle). Fill each muffin cup halfway with the pasta, coiling it into a circle, and top with about a tablespoon of the cheese (you should use about half of the 6 ounces). Fill each cup nearly to the top with the egg mixture. Bake the flans in a 350°F oven until they are thoroughly done in the center and lightly browned, about 25 minutes. Remove from the oven, let cool until they are easy to handle, and remove them from the tins. If you are making them in advance, refrigerate the flans and let them come to room temperature before serving.

Meanwhile, make the dressing by placing the egg yolk, lemon juice, anchovies, mustard, and garlic in a food processor. Pulse until the ingredients are well blended. With the motor running, add the olive oil slowly, followed by the cheese and pepper. Taste the dressing and add salt if necessary.

To serve, first grill or toast the bread, brush it with a bit of olive oil, and season it with salt and pepper. Set the bread—now large croutons—aside. Clean the romaine lettuce, discarding any damaged outer leaves. Divide the tender, inner leaves among 6 salad plates. Using a sharp knife, cut the good outer leaves into thin, crosswise strips about $\frac{1}{4}$ inch wide. Place 2 flans on each plate and stand 1 crouton between them. Add the lettuce strips, then spoon the dressing over both the leaves and the flan. Dust each salad with the remaining 3 ounces grated cheese and a couple of turns of black pepper and serve.

Composed Salad with Chicken, Angel Hair Pasta, & Preserved Lemons

Serves 4 to 6 as a main course

One of my culinary students deserves credit for this dish. While I was working on the manuscript, she brought me a jar of her caper-anchovy dressing. With one taste, this salad sprang into my head, nearly fully formed. I gathered the ingredients, called a couple of friends, and we all agreed that this hearty main-dish salad has an intriguing and delicious interplay of flavors and textures evocative of Caesar salad. Although I think the anchovies in the dressing are essential, the other ingredients can be varied to suit almost any dietary preference or requirement. The pancetta or chicken can be omitted and olives can be added.

6 ounces imported capel-
  lini (angel hair pasta) or
  spaghettini
Juice of 1 lemon, or less
About 2 tablespoons extra
  virgin olive oil

¼ pound pancetta or
  bacon, diced
1 to 1½ pounds cooked
  chicken meat
1 head romaine lettuce

CAPER-DIJON DRESSING:

1 tablespoon Dijon mustard
1 tablespoon drained capers
1 tablespoon liquid from the capers
1 tablespoon fresh lemon juice
1 tablespoon anchovy paste, or 2 or 3 anchovy fillets

2 cloves garlic
2 tablespoons chopped fresh Italian parsley
$\frac{1}{4}$ cup extra virgin olive oil
$\frac{3}{4}$ cup pure olive oil
Freshly ground black pepper

2 to 3 ounces freshly grated Parmesan or romano cheese
2 tablespoons drained capers

2 to 3 tablespoons chopped Preserved Lemons with Mustard Seeds & Mustard Oil (page 196), plus several wedges preserved lemon for garnish
4 or 5 anchovy fillets (optional)
3 to 4 cups pepper croutons (see Note)

Bring a large pot of salted water to a boil. Add the pasta and cook until it is almost done. Drain, rinse with cool water, and let stand in the colander or sieve until all the water has drained off. Toss the pasta with just enough of the lemon juice and olive oil to coat it *lightly*. Season with salt and black pepper. Set aside.

Meanwhile, sauté the *pancetta* or bacon in a heavy skillet until it just begins to crisp, being careful not to burn it.

Cut the chicken into medium julienne and set aside.

Remove any damaged outer leaves and the core of the lettuce. Cut the lettuce crosswise into strips ¾ inch wide.

To make the dressing, place all of the ingredients except the olive oils and pepper in a food processor and pulse until well blended. With the motor running, add both oils in a thin, steady stream. Taste the dressing and season with black pepper. (The dressing can be made a day or two in advance and refrigerated; bring to room temperature before using.)

To assemble the salad, have all of the ingredients at hand. Select a large straight-sided clear glass bowl, if possible. If not, any large salad bowl will do. Begin to assemble the salad by placing half of the romaine lettuce in the bowl. Top with half the pasta. Arrange half of the chicken on top of the pasta, and top that first with half of the cheese, half of the *pancetta* or bacon, half of the capers, and half of the chopped preserved lemon, arranging each ingredient over the entire surface. Pour half of the dressing over the salad. Repeat the process with the remaining ingredients. Complete the salad by topping it first with wedges of preserved lemon, then the anchovy fillets, if using, and finally the croutons. Serve immediately. It is not necessary to toss the salad to serve it. Simply use a large serving fork and serving spoon to extend down into the bowl and pull out each portion.

Note: To make pepper croutons, place about ¾ cup of extra virgin olive oil in a large jar that has a lid. Add four cups of cubed sourdough bread, fresh or day-old, close the container, and shake it until the bread has absorbed all the oil and the cubes are evenly coated. Add 2 teaspoons of freshly ground black pepper and shake the container until it has been evenly distributed. Place the bread cubes on a baking sheet and bake in a 250°F oven until the croutons are golden and dry. Cool, use immediately, or store in an airtight container.

Summer Potato Salad with Radishes & Green Beans

Serves 6

I find the addition of radishes and green beans to this salad very refreshing. Tiny haricots verts are wonderful, and it is worth the effort it takes to find them (or grow them, if you are blessed with garden space).

2 pounds small new
potatoes, unpeeled
¾ pound green beans
(haricots verts or Blue
Lakes), trimmed
1 bunch radishes, trimmed
1 bunch green onions,
trimmed

Lemon-Mustard Vinai-
grette (page 184)
Salt and freshly ground
black pepper
4 hard-boiled eggs
(optional)
Mustard Cream (page
186, optional)

Wash the potatoes. If they are very small, cut them in half; if not, cut them in quarters. Boil them until they are just tender, rinse and drain them, and place them in a large bowl.

Unless using *haricots verts*, cut the beans into 1½-inch lengths. Plunge them into rapidly boiling water and cook until tender but not overcooked, about 5 minutes. Rinse and drain them and add them to the bowl with the potatoes. Slice the radishes very thinly and chop the green onions into small rounds. Add them both to the potatoes. Add ¾ cup of the vinaigrette to the mixture and toss lightly. Taste the salad and correct the seasoning with salt and pepper.

If using the hard-boiled eggs, slice 2 of them and toss

with the other vegetables. Place the salad in an attractive serving bowl. Cut the remaining 2 eggs into quarters and arrange them on top of the salad. Top each slice of egg with a dollop of the mustard cream. Dust the entire surface with pepper.

VARIATION:
Grill several of your favorite Italian sausages. Cool them and then slice and toss with the salad.

Potato Salad with Italian Salami, Olives, & Arugula

Serves 6

This is an excellent salad for a picnic—hearty, flavorful, and easy to transport. Just carry the cleaned arugula separately so that it doesn't wilt.

2 pounds very small new red potatoes, unpeeled
1/2 pound very good Italian salami (soprassatta is especially good), sliced
3/4 cup pitted Kalamata or Niçoise olives
3/4 cup pure olive oil

2 tablespoons red wine vinegar
Juice of 1 lemon
3 tablespoons Dijon mustard
Salt and freshly ground black pepper
2 bunches arugula

Wash the potatoes, cut them in half, and cook in boiling water until tender, about 7 to 12 minutes, depending on size. Rinse in cold water, drain, and let cool.

Cut the salami into thin strips and toss it and the olives with the potatoes. Whisk together the olive oil, vinegar, lemon juice, and mustard, add salt and pepper to taste, pour over potato mixture, and toss.

Arrange the arugula on a serving platter and mound the potato salad on top.

VARIATION:
Instead of the dressing listed here, use the Mustard-Anchovy Vinaigrette on page 184.

Bread & Sausage Salad

Serves 6 to 8

Bread salad has no rules except for one: Use the best bread you can find. Other than that, the variations are endless. It is a great way to use up good-quality leftovers (roasted chicken, for example) or too many garden vegetables at harvest. I created this version to echo one of life's simplest culinary pleasures: good sausage on great bread slathered with the best mustard. This salad captures the spirit in a rustic mix that is easy to serve and easy to take along to the beach, park, or hiking trail. If you plan to transport it, keep the sliced sausages in a separate container that will keep them warm, and add them just before eating.

6 cups day-old bread (a good, country-style french or Italian bread is essential), cut into 1 ½-inch cubes
Mustard Vinaigrette (page 183)
1 pound spicy sausages (andouille or Sicilian)
1 medium red onion, diced
1 teaspoon finely minced garlic (about 4 cloves)
1 tablespoon yellow mustard seeds
Salt and freshly ground black pepper

Toss the bread with half the vinaigrette and let sit for 30 minutes.

Broil, grill, or fry the sausages until they are done, and then drain on absorbent paper. Cut into small rounds and keep warm. Toss the bread with the red onion, garlic, and mustard seeds. Add the sausage and the remaining dressing and toss again. Taste the salad, add salt and pepper as needed, and serve.

Chick-pea Salad with Mustard-Anchovy Vinaigrette

Serves 4 to 6

Here familiar ingredients merge in an unusual combination that works very well. The intensity of the vinaigrette draws all the elements together in a wonderful play of taste and texture.

1 cup dried chick-peas, soaked in water overnight

6 ounces haricot verts (if available) or Blue Lake green beans

4 ounces small dry pasta (such as tripolini, ditalini, small shells)

1 bunch radishes, cut into small julienne and held in ice water

1 bunch green onions, very thinly sliced

3 to 4 ounces good-quality cooked ham, torn into medium shreds (optional)

¼ cup Kalamata olives, pitted and coarsely chopped

2 cloves garlic, minced

Mustard-Anchovy Vinaigrette (see variations, page 184)

Drain, rinse, cook the chick-peas in water to cover until just tender, and let cool. Plunge the green beans into boiling water, cook 6 or 7 minutes, rinse, and hold in ice water. If you have not already done so, make the vinaigrette while you cook the pasta until it is just tender. Rinse the pasta in cool water and drain.

Drain the green beans and the radishes. In a large

bowl, toss together all the ingredients except the dressing. Add the vinaigrette, toss again, and serve immediately. If you must hold this salad in the refrigerator, it should be brought to room temperature and tossed before serving.

Bistro Salad Plate

Serves 4 to 6

Each time I visit New York City, I stop by the Manhattan Bistro on Spring Street in Soho. It is lively and unpretentious, and always has good red wine by the glass. One day, I was thrilled to see céleri rémoulade on the menu, happier still that it was accompanied by beets in a light vinaigrette. My elaboration upon that simple lunch is a satisfying meal in itself, full of very pleasant taste and texture contrasts. Serve with good hot bread and a fruity red wine.

2 bunches (about 6 beets each) baby beets, golden, pink, or red
1 tablespoon mustard oil or extra virgin olive oil
Salt and freshly ground black pepper
Spicy Glazed Carrots (page 137)
Céleri Rémoulade (page 136), or Celery Root,

Fennel, Apple, & Radish Salad (page 147)
$\frac{1}{2}$ cup (2 ounces) walnut halves, toasted
3 ounces Roquefort cheese or Oregon blue cheese, crumbled
Mustard flowers (if in season) or fresh Italian parsley sprigs for garnish

Trim the beets, leaving on a bit of stem to avoid bleeding, and cook them in boiling water until tender but not mushy.

Drain, rinse in cold water, and set them aside to cool. If you have not already done so, prepare the glazed carrots and the celery root. Peel the beets. Cut them into sixths, toss them with the oil, and season with salt and pepper. Toss them again with the walnuts and blue cheese.

On one large serving platter or on 4 to 6 individual serving plates, arrange the 3 vegetables in separate, attractive piles. Garnish with the mustard flowers or parsley.

Seared Orange Slices with Mustard & Arugula

Serves 4

I particularly like the sweetness of the oranges with the crisp, pleasant bitterness of the arugula. The sweet sauce with its subtle mustard undertones ties the two together beautifully. For a more substantial, main-dish salad, grill or broil two chicken or duck breasts, slice them, and serve them alongside the seared oranges.

2 tablespoons pure olive oil
4 to 6 blood oranges (preferably) or navel oranges, peeled, and cut into slices 1/4 inch thick
Freshly ground black pepper

3/4 cup blood-orange juice or other fresh orange juice
1 tablespoon low-salt soy sauce
1 to 2 teaspoons Dijon mustard
1 bunch (about 1 quart) young arugula, washed and trimmed

Heat the olive oil in a heavy skillet until very hot. Add the orange slices, just a few at a time, being sure not to crowd the pan. Sear quickly, turn, and sear on the second side, for a total cooking time of just 45 to 60 seconds. Transfer the seared oranges to a warmed plate and continue until all the orange slices are cooked. Sprinkle the oranges with several turns of the pepper mill and keep them warm.

Pour the orange juice into the skillet and deglaze the pan over medium heat. Add the soy sauce and reduce by one half. Stir in the mustard to taste and pour the sauce over the oranges. Serve immediately with the arugula leaves on the side.

Warm Cabbage Salad with Goat Cheese, Spicy Toasted Pecans, & Maple-Mustard Dressing

Serves 4

Although good cabbage is available all year long, I prefer this sweet-and-savory salad in the winter, when its richness is warm and comforting.

1 teaspoon hot mustard flour (or Colman's dry mustard)
1 teaspoon water
1 small head red cabbage
½ pound pancetta or good-quality bacon
½ cup extra virgin olive oil
2 cloves garlic, minced
1 tablespoon maple syrup, honey, or light molasses
2 tablespoons Dijon mustard
3 tablespoons apple cider vinegar
Salt and freshly ground black pepper
5 ounces chabis or young, fresh chèvre
Spicy Toasted Pecans (page 198)

Mix the mustard flour and cold water and set it aside for 20 minutes. Core and finely shred the cabbage and set it aside.

Cook the *pancetta* or bacon until just crisp and transfer it to absorbent paper to cool; reserve the drippings.

Meanwhile, whisk together the olive oil, 2 tablespoons of the pan drippings, the garlic, the sweetener, the mustard, and the vinegar. Taste and correct the seasoning with salt and pepper. Heat half the dressing and toss the cabbage in the pan with the dressing to warm it through. Transfer the cabbage to a serving platter or 4 individual plates. Crumble the goat cheese and the bacon over the cabbage. Spoon the remaining dressing over the top and sprinkle with the pecans. Serve immediately.

MUSTARDS

Making mustard in your own kitchen can be quite reward-
ing. It is fun, relatively easy, and can result in some delicious, inexpensive condiments that will serve you well. It is
important to keep in mind, however, that you will be limited
in the results you can achieve. I am particularly fond of the
texture of imported Dijon mustards, and it is not possible, as
I have discovered both through trial and error and through
lengthy discussions with professional mustard makers, to
duplicate that texture at home. We simply do not have the
equipment. Dijon mustards frequently go through further
grinding after they have been blended, a process that gives
many of them such a velvety texture. In setting out to make
Dijon-style mustard in your own kitchen, keep this in mind
from the start or you may be disappointed with the results.

Another difficulty with making mustards at home is
lack of access to quality raw materials. Finding good mustard flour is not easy, and the labeling of what we do find is
often vague or inaccurate. In most markets, mustard flour is
generally labeled dry mustard, but the type—white or
brown, mild or hot—is not always included. For this reason,
Colman's dry mustard is a dependable choice. Because it is a
mix of both white and brown mustard flours, it provides
mustard's full range of flavor and pungency. If you know a
wholesale restaurant outlet, you may be able to find products labeled dry mustard, mild, and dry mustard, hot. These
generally indicate white mustard and brown mustard, re-

spectively, and will allow you to use the two varieties as you wish. The recipes call for mustard flour by weight, which is how you will be purchasing your mustard. Because most of us measure ingredients by volume, however, the approximate volume measurement is also provided.

Following a few essential rules when using mustard flour will help ensure success. A simple understanding of the chemistry of mustard is important. Its heat and flavor are due to a chemical reaction that takes place between components in the mustard when they come in contact with oxygen and *water.* Many recipes call for mixing dry mustard directly with an acid or other liquid, but I believe this inhibits the full development of mustard's flavor and heat. I recommend mixing all dry mustard with enough very cold water to make a paste. A warm liquid will make a mustard bitter if it is introduced before the chemical reaction is complete. Next, the mixture should sit for 20 minutes, the amount of time it takes for the chemical reaction to reach its peak. The mustard paste can then be used in any recipe. Although I chill all liquid ingredients before adding them to the mustard paste, it is not absolutely necessary. After completing a homemade mustard recipe, the mustard must be allowed to age. Generally, I prefer two to four weeks of aging on the pantry shelf; in that time the mustard will have mellowed and all the flavors will have blended harmoniously. To preserve this balance, I then refrigerate the mustard. Some recipes recommend aging mustards in the refrigerator, but I find this results in an unbalanced product.

Cold liquids should also be used with mustard seeds so that the same essential chemical reaction can take place. All seeds must be soaked for several hours before you attempt to grind them in a food processor or blender, although they can be crushed, completely dry, with a mortar and pestle.

Another way to make mustards at home is to begin with a good Dijon mustard and develop your own flavorings and seasonings. The use of commercial Dijon mustards has certain advantages, although it is not necessarily as satisfying as starting from scratch. Primarily, it allows you to make a flavored mustard and use it immediately, without the aging that is required if you begin with mustard flour. I recommend some of my favorite versions here, and it is easy and fairly inexpensive to experiment to find your own favorites. Keep in mind that once you introduce anything other than dried spices into mustard, you are probably shortening its shelf life. Fresh herbs—which must be blanched or they will not hold their color—introduce vegetable matter and additional moisture, making your mustard more perishable than it originally was. For this reason, mustards that you flavor yourself should be kept in the refrigerator and used within a week or ten days to ensure maximum flavor.

Dijon-Style Mustard, Version I

Makes about 2 pints

As this mustard ages, it becomes quite smooth and mellow, although it never approaches the delicate texture of the best commercial mustards. Be sure to read the introduction to making mustards at home (page 164) before you begin.

6 ounces (1 ½ cups) hot mustard flour (or Colman's dry mustard)
½ cup very cold water
2 cups apple cider vinegar, medium acid
2 cups dry white wine
1 yellow onion, minced
5 large shallots, minced
6 cloves garlic, minced
2 bay leaves
1 large fresh tarragon sprig
1 teaspoon fresh chervil leaves
15 whole black peppercorns
8 whole juniper berries
¼ cup fresh lemon juice, chilled
1 tablespoon kosher salt
1 tablespoon sugar

Make a paste of the mustard flour and water and set it aside. Place the vinegar, wine, onion, shallots, garlic, bay leaves, tarragon, chervil, peppercorns, and juniper berries in a heavy, nonreactive saucepan. Simmer the mixture over medium heat until it is reduced by two thirds, and then strain it, cover, and chill.

When the vinegar reduction is cold, stir it into the mustard paste, along with the lemon juice, salt, and sugar. Let stand for at least 20 minutes; the mixture will gradually thicken and the mustard will begin to mellow. Simmer over low heat for another 15 minutes. Remove from the heat and let cool. Bottle it, cap tightly, and store on a dark, cool shelf for at least 4 weeks, or for up to 6 weeks, before using. Refrigerate it once you begin using it. Its flavor should hold for up to 6 months.

# Dijon-Style Mustard, Version II

Makes about 1 pint

This Dijon-style mustard is somewhat more time consuming than Version I, but it is a good example of how to make a finished mustard from whole seeds.

½ pound (8 ounces) brown mustard seeds

2 cups (1 pint) chilled unsweetened juice from white grapes, or as needed

3 cloves garlic, crushed

1 tablespoon whole black peppercorns, slightly crushed by hand

6 whole cloves

1-inch piece of fresh ginger, peeled and chopped

3 tablespoons fresh chervil leaves

1 tablespoon fresh tarragon leaves, chopped

2 bay leaves

1 teaspoon fresh thyme leaves

1-inch piece of cinnamon

½ teaspoon freshly grated nutmeg

2 teaspoons kosher salt

Place all of the ingredients except the salt in a large bowl or jar and cover with a cloth towel. Let the mixture sit for 2 days at room temperature, checking it occasionally to make sure the seeds are completely submerged in the liquid. As the seeds absorb liquid, you may need to add more grape juice.

After 2 days, place the seed mixture in a food processor and grind it as fine as possible. Strain the mixture through a stainless-steel sieve, using a pestle to push it through. Strain the mixture a second time through a finer sieve. Store it in 2 tightly capped half-pint jars in a cool dark place for 4 to 6 weeks before using.

Transfer the mustard to the refrigerator once you begin using it. Its flavor should hold for up to 6 months.

Red Wine Mustard

Makes about 1½ pints

Pale pink rather than red, this is a hearty homemade mustard with a rich and complex flavor. Be sure to allow enough time for aging; tasted too quickly, this mustard is rough and unbalanced.

4 ounces (1 cup) hot mustard flour (or Colman's dry mustard)
½ cup very cold water
1¼ cups red wine vinegar, low or medium acid
1¼ cups hearty red wine
1 yellow onion, minced
5 large shallots, minced
6 cloves garlic, minced
2 bay leaves
1 large fresh tarragon sprig

1 teaspoon fresh chervil leaves
¼-inch piece cinnamon stick
15 whole black peppercorns
8 whole juniper berries
1 tablespoon kosher salt
1 tablespoon sugar
1 teaspoon freshly ground white pepper

Make a paste of the mustard flour and water and set it aside.
Simmer all the ingredients except the salt, sugar, and

pepper in a heavy, nonreactive saucepan over medium heat until reduced by two thirds. Strain the reduced liquid, cover, and chill. Once it is cold, stir it into the mustard paste, along with the salt, sugar, and pepper, and then simmer the mixture over low heat for 15 minutes, or until it begins to thicken. Remove from the heat and let cool. Pour into half-pint jars, cap tightly, and store on a cool, dark shelf for 4 to 6 weeks. Refrigerate it after the first use. It will retain its flavor for 6 months.

Raspberry Mustard

Makes about ¾ pint

This mustard is similar to the homemade Dijon-style mustards, but with a slightly sweeter element and a subtle undertaste of raspberry that is quite nice.

2 ounces (½ cup) hot mustard flour (or Colman's dry mustard)

2 tablespoons very cold water

1 cup raspberry vinegar, low or medium acid

½ cup dry white wine

1 yellow onion, chopped

2 shallots, chopped

5 cloves garlic, minced

2 tablespoons fresh lemon juice, chilled

2 teaspoons kosher salt

2 teaspoons sugar

½ teaspoon freshly ground white pepper

Mix the mustard flour with the water and set it aside. In a nonreactive saucepan, simmer the vinegar, wine, onion, shallots, and garlic over medium heat until reduced by two thirds. Strain the mixture, cover, and chill. When cold, mix it with the mustard paste, and stir in the lemon juice, salt, sugar, and pepper. Simmer over low heat for 15 minutes. Remove from the heat, let cool, and then place in glass jars. Cap tightly and store in a cool, dark place for at least 3 weeks before using. After the first use, store in the refrigerator, where its flavor will hold for up to 6 months.

Coarse-Grain Mustard with Beer

Makes about 1 to 1½ pints

This is an excellent mustard, easy to make and full of good flavor. I find it rivals all but the very best commercial coarse-grain mustards, and I particularly enjoy the spicy variation.

1 cup dark beer, chilled
½ cup yellow mustard seeds
1½ cups apple cider vinegar, medium acid
1 small yellow onion (preferably sweet), chopped
5 to 6 cloves garlic, minced
1 shallot, chopped

2 ounces (½ cup) hot mustard flour (or Colman's dry mustard)
2 tablespoons very cold water
1½ teaspoons kosher salt
2 teaspoons sugar
½ teaspoon ground allspice

Pour the dark beer over the mustard seed and let it sit at least 4 hours or overnight. Place the vinegar, onion, garlic, and shallot in a heavy, nonreactive saucepan and simmer slowly over medium heat until mixture is reduced by two thirds. Strain the liquid, cover, and chill.

Meanwhile, make a paste of the mustard flour and water and let it sit for 20 minutes. Then stir in the cold vinegar reduction, salt, sugar, and allspice and add the wet mustard seeds.

Place the mixture in a food processor and pulse until the mustard seeds are partially ground and the mixture is well blended. Transfer the mustard to the saucepan and simmer over very low heat until it thickens, 10 to 15 minutes. Cool the mixture, place in a glass jar, cap tightly, and age on a cool, dark shelf for 2 or 3 weeks before using. It will retain its flavor for up to 6 months if refrigerated after the first use.

VARIATION:

SPICY COARSE-GRAIN MUSTARD: Along with the salt, sugar, and allspice, add ⅛ teaspoon ground cardamom, ¼ teaspoon each of ground cinnamon and ground clove, ½ teaspoon ground cumin, 1 teaspoon grated fresh ginger, and 2 tablespoons very finely minced candied ginger.

Chinese-Style Mustard

Makes about ½ cup

This is the condiment traditionally served in Asian restaurants in North America. It should be made fresh, about thirty minutes before serving.

2 ounces (½ cup) hot mustard flour (or Colman's dry mustard)	**Very cold water**

In a glass or ceramic bowl, stir enough water into the mustard flour to make a paste. Let it sit for 20 minutes, and then add water as needed to make the consistency you want.

The Devil's Mustard

Makes about ½ to ¾ cup

I came up with this mustard by accident. When I was first testing recipes, I experimented by mixing mild mustard flour and hot mustard flour with a variety of liquids, just to see what would result. I thought I was being frivolous when I mixed some hot mustard flour with nothing but Tabasco sauce, but I actually liked the combination a great deal. This mixture can be used right away, as part of a sausage and mustard buffet, perhaps, or with any grilled poultry or meat. But be assured, it is hot.

3 ounces (¾ cup) hot mustard flour (or Colman's dry mustard)
2 tablespoons very cold water

⅛ cup Tabasco sauce
2 cloves garlic, pressed
1 teaspoon kosher salt

Mix the mustard flour and water to make a paste and let it sit for 20 minutes. Stir in the Tabasco sauce, garlic, and salt.

Honey Mustard

Makes about 1 pint

Honey mustard is wonderful on sandwiches, with roast poultry, or as an element of a more complex sauce.

4 ounces (1 cup) hot mustard flour (or Colman's dry mustard)
1/4 cup very cold water

1/2 cup rice wine vinegar
1/4 cup honey
2 cloves garlic, pressed
1 teaspoon kosher salt

Make a paste of the mustard flour and water and let it sit for 20 minutes. Stir in the other ingredients, place the mixture in a glass jar, cap tightly, and store on a dark, cool shelf for 3 weeks before using. If the mustard is refrigerated after the first use, the flavor will hold up for 3 months.

Note: Honey contains the spores of the bacterium *Clostridium botulinum*, which can cause fatal food poisoning. It is not safe to give honey to small children, because the acidic environment of a child's stomach, unlike that of an adult's, may not be strong enough to combat the bacterium.

Honey-Pepper Mustard

Makes about 3/4 cup

I love the combination of honey, garlic, and pepper and use it frequently in a variety of recipes. Here the ingredients come together with mustard to create an enticing mixture that is great in any recipe that calls for a simple honey mustard.

2 ounces (1/2 cup) hot mustard flour (or Colman's dry mustard)
1/4 cup very cold water
2 tablespoons imported sherry vinegar

2 tablespoons honey (see Note in preceding recipe)
3 cloves garlic, pressed
1 tablespoon freshly ground black pepper
1 teaspoon kosher salt

Make a paste of the mustard flour and water and let it sit for 20 minutes. Then stir in the remaining ingredients, place the mustard into a glass or porcelain jar, cap tightly, and let rest in a cool, dark cupboard for 2 to 3 weeks before using. Refrigerate the mustard once you begin using it.

Honey-Ginger Mustard

Makes approximately 1 cup

I love the element contributed by the candied ginger in this smooth, sweet mixture. I use this mustard in a variety of recipes and find it is especially good as a dip when mixed with the All-Purpose Mustard Sauce on page 188. Because the base of this mustard is prepared Dijon, lengthy aging is not required. I find the mustard is fine for use after allowing it to rest for a day. Do store it in the refrigerator, however, so that it maintains its peak of flavor.

2 tablespoons hot mustard flour (or Colman's dry mustard)
1 tablespoon very cold water
¾ cup Dijon mustard

5 tablespoons honey (see Note, page 174)
¼ cup candied ginger, very finely chopped
1 teaspoon grated fresh ginger

Mix the mustard flour with the water to form a smooth paste. Let it sit for 20 minutes. Put the mustard paste, Dijon mustard, honey, and both gingers in a food processor. Pulse until the mixture is smooth. Store in a glass jar in the refrigerator.

 Sun-Drenched Mustard

Makes about 1 cup

The combination of good Dijon mustard and sun-dried tomatoes is quite intense. Use this mustard on sandwiches, roast tomatoes, or grilled chicken or fish.

¾ cup Dijon mustard
¼ cup sun-dried tomatoes, packed in oil, drained, and puréed
1 shallot
1 teaspoon fresh oregano leaves, blanched (see Note below)

Several fresh Italian parsley sprigs, blanched and large stems removed (see Note)

Place all ingredients in a food processor and pulse until very smooth. Store, refrigerated, in a glass jar.

Note: Blanch fresh herbs by plunging them into a pot of rapidly boiling water for 15 seconds. Transfer them from the boiling water to a bowl of ice water for 15 seconds. Drain the herbs and pat them dry between the folds of a tea towel.

Jalapeño-Cilantro Mustard

Makes about ¾ cup

Here, mustard provides a new dimension to the traditional Mexican combination of jalapeño peppers and cilantro. This mustard is outstanding with seafood, especially grilled tuna, swordfish, and shark, and is also quite good with black beans, grilled and broiled chicken, and most types of sausages.

1 bunch cilantro, blanched and stems removed (see Note in preceding recipe)

1 teaspoon hot mustard flour (or Colman's dry mustard), mixed with 1 teaspoon very cold water

¾ cup extra-forte Dijon mustard

1 jalapeño pepper, stemmed, seeded, and coarsely chopped

2 cloves garlic

Place the cilantro, mustard flour, Dijon mustard, jalapeño pepper, and garlic in a food processor and pulse until the mixture is very smooth. Transfer to a glass bowl or jar. Cover tightly and refrigerate until ready to use.

Cilantro-Mint Mustard

Makes about ¾ cup

I love the combination of flavors in this mustard and find it is a wonderful condiment for any type of seafood, especially grilled tuna, halibut, or shark.

2 tablespoons fresh cilantro, blanched and finely minced (see Note, page 177)

2 tablespoons fresh mint, blanched and finely minced (see Note, page 177)

2 cloves garlic
Juice of 1 lime
½ to ¾ cup Dijon mustard

Place the cilantro, mint, garlic, and lime juice in a food processor and pulse several times to mix well. Add ½ cup of the mustard and pulse until well blended. Taste the mixture and add the remaining mustard if you prefer the flavor of the herbs to be less pronounced. Store in a jar in the refrigerator.

Sage-Shallot Mustard

Makes about ¾ cup

Make this savory mustard during the winter holidays and use it on turkey sandwiches.

3 tablespoons fresh sage leaves, blanched (see Note, page 177)

1 shallot

1 teaspoon freshly ground black pepper

½ to ¾ cup Dijon mustard

Place the sage and shallot in a food processor and pulse until finely chopped. Add the black pepper and ½ cup of the mustard and pulse again until the mixture is fairly smooth (it will remain slightly chunky). Taste the mixture and add the additional mustard for a milder taste. Store in a jar in the refrigerator for 1 day before using, to allow the flavors to blend.

Three-Olive Mustard

Makes about ¾ cup

This mustard is a real treat on tuna sandwiches or with tuna salads. It is also excellent on bruschetta (Italian-style grilled bread), on sandwiches made with ripe summer tomatoes, and with all types of grilled vegetables.

1 tablespoon finely minced pitted California black olives

1 tablespoon finely minced Kalamata olives

1 tablespoon finely minced pitted green olives or Italian-style dried olives

1 clove garlic, finely minced

½ to ¾ cup Dijon mustard

By hand or in a food processor, mix together all of the ingredients, using the smaller amount of mustard if a more intense flavor of olives is desired. Store in a jar in the refrigerator.

Olive-Anchovy Mustard

Makes about ¾ cup

Anchovy lovers will adore this mustard and find all sorts of uses for it. I think it is excellent on sandwiches of grilled eggplant, roasted sweet peppers, and mozzarella cheese. It is also outstanding with boiled new potatoes and red onion and with grilled or roasted vegetables.

2 tablespoons finely minced pitted California black olives

1 tablespoon finely minced pitted Kalamata olives

2 to 4 anchovy fillets

1 tablespoon blanched and minced fresh Italian parsley (see Note, page 177)

½ to ¾ cup Dijon mustard

Combine the olives, 2 anchovy fillets, and the parsley in a food processor and pulse until well blended. Add ½ cup of the mustard and pulse until fairly smooth. Taste the mixture and add additional anchovies for a stronger flavor or the additional mustard for a milder anchovy flavor. Store in a jar in the refrigerator.

Roasted-Garlic Mustard

Makes about ¾ cup

This is a tender, delicate mustard that makes an elegant accompaniment to roast chicken, pork, and all types of seafood. It is also excellent on good crusty bread, topped with ripe tomatoes and fresh garlic, or on sandwiches of all types.

3 tablespoons roasted
  garlic purée (See
  Note, page 142)
2 teaspoons fresh thyme
  leaves, blanched (see
  Note, page 177)

1 teaspoon freshly ground
  black pepper
½ cup Dijon mustard

Place all of the ingredients in a food processor and pulse until smooth. Store in a jar in the refrigerator.

Smoky Hot Mustard

Makes about 1 cup

The long, slow heat of chipotle peppers is a real treat. You might try this mustard with the Grilled Tuna with Black Beans on page 96 or as one of several condiments with grilled sausages.

¾ cup Dijon mustard
1 canned chipotle pepper
  in adobo sauce, plus 1
  teaspoon of the sauce
  (see Note)

2 tablespoons tomato
  purée
1 teaspoon kosher salt
  (omit if the Dijon mus-
  tard is particularly salty)

Combine all the ingredients in a food processor and pulse until very smooth. Store in a jar in the refrigerator.

Note: *Chipotle* peppers are ripened, smoked jalapeño peppers. Look for them canned in *adobo* sauce in specialty shops and most Hispanic markets.

Mustard Vinaigrette

Makes about 1½ cups

Many vinaigrette dressings list mustard—generally flour or Dijon—in their ingredients, using it as one of several flavoring agents where it plays a subtle rather than dominant role. There are other vinaigrettes, mixtures where mustard is the predominant flavor, and those are the ones that I believe deserve the designation mustard vinaigrette *and are the ones of which I speak here.*

Mustard vinaigrette can be made quickly and simply, just before you are ready to toss it with your favorite greens or pasta, or spoon it over a baked potato, steamed asparagus, or a grilled chicken sandwich. It is a simple mixture of a good oil, preferably olive, your preferred acid (I like lemon juice), your favorite Dijon mustard, and a little salt and pepper. If all your ingredients are readily at hand, the mixture can be whisked together in under a minute.

The variations are countless: Change the type of mustard, the acid—red wine vinegar, white wine vinegar, sherry vinegar, balsamic vinegar, lime juice—the type of oil, and the herbs, spices, and seasonings. Add garlic or omit it; mash anchovies and mix them in. Add honey, capers, or sun-dried tomatoes.

This version is a basic vinaigrette, slightly more complex than a simple mixture of oil, mustard, and acid, and a good backdrop for other flavors. Consider the variations listed at the end of the recipe, or devise your own. Other mustard vinaigrettes appear throughout the book, paired with specific recipes but good with other foods, too.

2 tablespoons Dijon
  mustard
1 shallot, minced
2 cloves garlic, minced
1 teaspoon finely chopped
  fresh thyme
1 teaspoon finely chopped
  Italian parsley
1/2 teaspoon freshly
  ground black pepper

1/2 teaspoon kosher salt
1 to 2 teaspoons hot
  mustard flour (or Col-
  man's dry mustard)
2 tablespoons Champagne
  vinegar
Juice of 1 lemon (3 to 4
  tablespoons)
1/2 cup extra virgin olive oil
1 cup pure olive oil

Place the Dijon mustard, shallot, garlic, and herbs in a mixing bowl and whisk together. Add the pepper and salt and blend. Mix the mustard flour with the vinegar and the lemon juice, and whisk the mixture into the Dijon mustard mixture. Slowly whisk in both olive oils. Taste and adjust the seasonings as desired.

VARIATIONS:

LEMON-MUSTARD VINAIGRETTE: Omit the vinegar and increase the quantity of lemon juice to taste.

MUSTARD-ANCHOVY VINAIGRETTE: Omit the lemon juice and Champagne vinegar. Crush 3 or 4 anchovy fillets in 5 tablespoons of red wine vinegar (medium acid) and use in their place.

Mustard Butter

Makes about ½ cup

Mustard butter has numerous and varied uses, so it is handy to have on hand. If you use it frequently, consider doubling the recipe and freezing half. It's good in emergencies, when you need to put together a meal quickly. Toss it with pasta; use it to flavor a grilled cheese sandwich, broiled chicken, fish, or tomatoes; or serve it with potatoes prepared in almost any fashion.

¼ pound unsalted butter at room temperature
3 tablespoons Dijon mustard
1 shallot, chopped

1 clove garlic, chopped
2 teaspoons chopped fresh Italian parsley
Salt and freshly ground black pepper

Blend the butter and mustard either in a food processor or with a fork. If you are using a processor, add the remaining ingredients and pulse until the butter is smooth. If you are mixing by hand, mince the shallot, garlic, and parsley together and combine with the butter mixture. Add the salt and a few turns of pepper to taste.

Mustard butter can be stored for several days in the refrigerator, but it must be covered. Place it in a crock, or roll it into a cylinder and enclose it in plastic wrap and chill it. It can then be sliced off in small, serving-sized rounds or coins.

VARIATIONS:

SINGLE HERB: Omit the parsley, and add 2 teaspoons of a different chopped, fresh herb. Sage, rosemary, thyme, dill, oregano, and basil are all particularly good, but keep in mind that with the addition of fresh vegetable matter—especially basil, because of its high water content—the butter becomes more perishable.

HERB BLENDS: Balanced mixtures of herbs are always good. Increase the total amount to 4 teaspoons fresh herbs, using 1 teaspoon of chopped Italian parsley, along with equal amounts of oregano, thyme, and marjoram.

CILANTRO: Omit the Italian parsley. Add 1 tablespoon chopped fresh cilantro, 1 teaspoon finely minced jalapeño or serrano pepper, and 2 teaspoons fresh lime juice.

GORGONZOLA BUTTER: Add 2 ounces imported Gorgonzola cheese and 2 teaspoons minced fresh rosemary to basic butter mixture.

# Mustard Cream

Makes about 1½ cups

This recipe is so versatile that I include it here to be used as a sauce for a variety of foods, not just the combinations that appear in this book. It is great as a dip for fresh vegetables or shrimp, and wonderful with a variety of salads. As a topping, it enhances soups, especially split pea and ham. Use it on potato salad, with fresh cracked crab, over avocadoes filled with smoked chicken and fennel, with grilled or broiled fish, with carpaccio or paté, *or alongside roast beef.*

1 cup sour cream mixed
  with ¼ cup half-and-
  half; or 1¼ cups crème
  fraîche

¼ cup Dijon mustard
1 teaspoon kosher salt
1 teaspoon freshly ground
  black pepper

Stir together the sour-cream mixture or *crème fraîche*, mustard, salt (omit the salt if the mustard is particularly salty), and pepper. Mustard cream may be made 2 or 3 days in advance. Cover and refrigerate until ready to use.

VARIATIONS:

This recipe can be varied to suit specific dishes. Using flavored mustard—green peppercorn or honey-ginger, for example—takes its deep flavors in a different direction than standard Dijon; different herbs add a more delicate shift in taste.

SAFFRON MUSTARD CREAM: Soak ½ teaspoon powdered saffron or 1 teaspoon saffron threads in 1 teaspoon warm water for 15 minutes. Stir the saffron mixture into the basic mustard cream and let it rest at least 1 hour before serving.

LEMON MUSTARD CREAM: Stir in the juice of ½ lemon. Meyer lemons, if available, are particularly good.

ORANGE MUSTARD CREAM: Stir in 2 to 3 tablespoons fresh orange juice, preferably from blood oranges, and 1 teaspoon grated orange zest.

ROSEMARY MUSTARD CREAM: Stir in 1 tablespoon very finely chopped fresh rosemary leaves; 1 clove garlic, pressed or finely minced; and 1 or 2 teaspoons fresh lemon juice.

CHIVE MUSTARD CREAM: Stir in the juice of $\frac{1}{2}$ lemon and 1 tablespoon snipped fresh chives.

FRESH HERB MUSTARD CREAM: Stir in 2 tablespoons finely chopped mixed fresh savory herbs of choice.

CILANTRO MUSTARD CREAM: Stir in the juice of $\frac{1}{2}$ lime and 2 tablespoons finely chopped fresh cilantro.

GREEN PEPPERCORN MUSTARD CREAM: Use green peppercorn mustard instead of Dijon, if possible. Rinse 2 tablespoons green peppercorns, crush them lightly, and stir into the basic mustard cream.

DILL MUSTARD CREAM: Stir in 1 tablespoon chopped fresh dill, 2 teaspoons dill seeds, and 1 teaspoon crushed celery seeds.

All-Purpose Mustard Sauce

Makes about 2 cups

Here is a handy condiment. It is practically indestructible, and keeps well in the refrigerator without any deterioration of flavor. On its own, it retains a great deal of heat, the sort of sinus-cleansing kind that reminds everyone who tries it of the Japanese horseradish called wasabi. *It forms an excellent base for a variety of sauces, especially dips for vegetables, seafood, breads, and the like. Simply add 3 or 4 tablespoons of your favorite flavored mustard to $\frac{1}{2}$ cup of the sauce and you have a flavorful dip with plenty of heat.*

4 ounces (1 cup) hot mustard flour (or Colman's dry mustard)
¼ cup apple cider vinegar, medium acid
¼ cup very cold water
1 tablespoon salt
¼ cup honey (see Note, page 174)
1 egg
1 cup pure olive oil

Stir together the mustard flour, vinegar, and water until the mixture is smooth. Add the salt and honey and stir again. Beat in the egg and then slowly add the olive oil, whisking constantly to form a smooth emulsion.

You can also make this condiment in a food processor. Place the mustard flour, water, vinegar, and salt in the processor. Pulse until evenly combined. Add the honey and egg and pulse again until the mixture is smooth. With the motor running, slowly drizzle in the olive oil and process until thick and smooth. Transfer the mixture to a container, cover, and refrigerate until ready to use.

Cranberry-Rhubarb Sauce

Makes about 3 cups

Use this sauce as a condiment with poultry, especially duck, turkey, and sausages. A quick version can be made by using 2 cups canned cranberry sauce in place of the fresh berries and omitting the sugar.

½ pound (about 2 cups) cranberries, cleaned, with bruised berries discarded
½ pound rhubarb, peeled and cut into 1-inch pieces
1 cup sugar
½ cup red wine or orange juice
½ teaspoon kosher salt
1 teaspoon freshly cracked black pepper
1 teaspoon very finely minced orange zest
1 to 2 tablespoons Dijon mustard

In a heavy, nonreactive saucepan, simmer the cranberries, rhubarb, and sugar over medium heat until the mixture is very soft, about 20 to 25 minutes. Purée with an immersion blender or in a food processor until smooth; then press through a sieve into a serving bowl.

Season with the salt, pepper, orange zest, and mustard to taste.

Plum-Mustard Sauce

Makes 1 to 1½ cups

This sweet-and-spicy condiment can be made with other fruits when plums, which have a fairly short season, are unavailable. The other ingredients work especially well with raspberries, peaches, and nectarines. The sauce is excellent served hot with roasted or grilled chicken or pork or with grilled sausages. Serve it with an array of other mustard condiments.

1 pound ripe plums
1 cup red wine (Beaujo-
    lais, Côte du Rhône, or
    Pinot Noir)
$\frac{1}{3}$ cup red wine vinegar,
    medium acid

$\frac{1}{3}$ cup sugar
$\frac{3}{4}$ teaspoon quatre épices
    (see page 206)
2 to 4 teaspoons Dijon
    mustard

Cut the plums from their stones and place them in a heavy, nonreactive saucepan, along with the wine, vinegar, sugar, and spices. Simmer over medium heat until the plums are very soft, about 15 minutes. Purée the mixture in a blender or food processor and return it to the saucepan, straining it first if you prefer a finer sauce. Simmer the mixture over low heat until it is reduced by about one fourth and begins to thicken. Stir in 2 teaspoons of the mustard, taste the mixture, and add additional mustard, a teaspoon at a time, to taste. The presence of the mustard should be subtle but unmistakable.

 # Dijon Pear Sauce

Makes approximately 2 cups

This sauce, guided by the delicate flavor of the pears, is more subtle than the Plum-Mustard Sauce (page 190) or the Cranberry-Rhubarb Sauce (page 189). It is elegant and understated and should be served with dishes that complement its delicacy, like the Gruyère Soufflé on page 84, or with the white meat of poultry, whose blandness will be brightened by these flavors. It can also be made with apricots, peaches, or apples, all fruits that pair nicely with white wine.

4 pears, peeled, cored,
   and coarsely chopped
¾ cup dry white wine
¼ cup white wine vinegar
   or apple cider vinegar,
   medium acid

3 whole cloves
Small piece of cinnamon
1 tablespoon Dijon
   mustard
Pinch of salt

Place the pears, wine, vinegar, cloves, and cinnamon in a nonreactive saucepan and simmer over medium heat until the pears are soft, approximately 10 minutes, depending on variety of pear. Remove the cloves and cinnamon and purée the mixture in an immersion blender or in a standard blender. Stir in the mustard and salt, taste, and adjust seasoning, adding more mustard if desired.

Mustard Bread Crumbs

Makes 3 cups

3 tablespoons butter
2 tablespoons Dijon
   mustard

3 cups fine dried bread
   crumbs (from french or
   Italian bread) (see Note)

Melt the butter in a large, heavy skillet. Remove from the heat, stir in the mustard, and add the bread crumbs, tossing to coat them well. Place the mixture in a 300°F oven until they are golden and lightly toasted, about 20 minutes. Remove from the oven, cool, and store in a closed container at room temperature until ready to use. They will keep for 10 days.

Note: To make bread crumbs easily, cut bread that is at least a day old into 1-inch cubes. Run them through a blender or processor, a large handful at a time, until they become small uniform crumbs.

Rhubarb-Strawberry Chutney with Mustard Seeds

Makes approximately 4 pints

1 pound (4 cups) rhubarb,
   peeled and cut into
   1-inch chunks

1 ½ cups brown sugar,
   firmly packed
1 ½ cups apple cider vinegar, medium acid

2-inch piece of fresh
   ginger, peeled and
   thinly sliced
1 or 2 jalapeño or serrano
   peppers, slit open
Several whole cloves
1-inch piece of cinnamon
   stick

3 tablespoons yellow
   mustard seeds
1 cup Zante currants
4 cups perfect strawber-
   ries, hulled and coarsely
   chopped

Place the rhubarb, brown sugar, vinegar, ginger, peppers, and spices in a large, nonreactive pot. Simmer over low heat until the rhubarb is very soft, 15 to 20 minutes. Add the currants and strawberries and simmer for an additional 5 minutes. Remove from the heat and let cool slightly.

Spoon into hot, sterilized half-pint or pint jars to within ½ inch of rim and seal jar according to manufacturer's directions. Process for 5 minutes in a boiling water bath. Store in a cool, dark cupboard. It will keep up to 1 year.

Mustard Pickle

Makes about 4 quarts

Homemade vegetable pickles are a real treat, and a great way to use extra garden vegetables. Both the mustard and the honey contribute unique elements to this version, as do the whole garlic cloves and sliced fennel. If you make this once, I guarantee it will become a favorite recipe. Vary the specific vegetables according to what is available when you make it.

1 pound small sweet
  onions, quartered
1 pound small pickling cucumbers, unpeeled, cut
  into rounds 1 inch thick
1 cup chopped sweet red
  peppers
1 cup whole garlic cloves,
  peeled
1 cup baby zucchini,
  trimmed but left whole
2 cups cauliflower florets
2 cups diagonally sliced
  carrots
2 cups large-julienned
  fennel
$\frac{1}{2}$ cup fresh jalapeño or
  serrano peppers, cut
  into rounds (optional)

$1\frac{1}{4}$ cups salt
5 cups apple cider vinegar,
  medium acid, chilled,
  with additional as
  needed to fill jars
$\frac{1}{2}$ cup hot mustard flour
  (or Colman's dry
  mustard)
$\frac{1}{2}$ cup all-purpose flour
1 cup honey (see Note,
  page 174)
1 tablespoon celery seeds
3 tablespoons white
  mustard seeds
1 tablespoon ground
  tumeric
1-inch cinnamon stick
1 teaspoon whole cloves

Place all the vegetables in a large, nonreactive container, using the chili peppers if you want a spicy pickle. Sprinkle
with the salt and add water to cover. Let sit overnight at
room temperature.

Mix the dry mustard with enough of the chilled vinegar to make a thin paste. Let it sit for 30 minutes. Stir the
all-purpose flour into the mustard paste and add the remaining vinegar, the honey, and all the spices. Simmer the mixture in a double boiler until it begins to thicken, about 8
minutes. Drain the vegetables, place them in a heavy, nonreactive pot, and pour the thickened mustard mixture over

them. Heat them through over medium heat. Ladle them into hot, sterilized jars, and, if necessary, add more apple cider vinegar to cover within ½ inch of the top of each jar. Process them for 5 minutes in a boiling-water bath. Seal according to manufacturer's directions and store in a cool, dark cupboard. They keep for up to 1 year.

Preserved Lemons with Mustard Seeds & Mustard Oil

Makes 1 pint

Because the entire lemon, skin and all, is used in this recipe, it is important to use lemons that have not been sprayed with pesticides or herbicides. These salty lemon slices, slivered or chopped, add spark to salsas, salads, and pasta dishes. Add a few to an antipasto platter, or simply snack on them, as I do.

3 or 4 organic lemons, preferably Meyer variety
¼ cup kosher salt
2 teaspoons sugar

2 teaspoons white mustard seeds
⅓ cup fresh lemon juice
Mustard oil or extra virgin olive oil

Wash the lemons and dry them thoroughly. Slice them lengthwise into sixths or eighths, depending on their size. In a nonreactive bowl, mix together the salt, sugar, and mustard seeds. Add the lemon slices and toss the mixture quickly to coat the lemons. Transfer the lemons to a clean pint jar and add the lemon juice. Cover the jar tightly and keep in a cool, dark cupboard for 7 days, turning it upside down each morning and righting it at night, so that all of the lemons spend time in the liquid.

On the seventh day, top off the jar with the oil. If you will be using the preserved lemons quickly, say within the month, there is no need to refrigerate them. You can hold them longer, but their flavor decreases after refrigeration.

Spicy Toasted Pecans

Makes about 2 cups

This was the hardest recipe in the book to test, especially as a part of a larger dish. These nuts are so good that I'd make them and eat them all within minutes. Yikes! What about chicken with a pecan crust, I'd tell myself, or that great salad with cabbage and goat cheese? Oh, well, if you have any left there are several great ways to use them. If not, enjoy!

½ pound pecans, shelled
2 tablespoons pure olive oil
¼ cup sugar
1 teaspoon hot mustard flour (or Colman's dry mustard)
1 teaspoon ground cinnamon
1 teaspoon ground ginger

1 teaspoon kosher salt
½ to 1 teaspoon freshly ground black pepper
¼ teaspoon ground cloves
¼ teaspoon ground cardamom
¼ teaspoon ground nutmeg
¼ teaspoon ground cumin

In a 275°F oven, toast the pecans on an ungreased baking sheet or in a heavy, ovenproof skillet, shaking or stirring occasionally, for 30 minutes.

While the nuts are toasting, mix the remaining ingredients together in a medium-sized bowl. Remove the nuts from the oven, toss them in the spice mixture, and spread them over the surface of the baking sheet or skillet. Increase the oven temperature to 375°F and toast for an additional 20 minutes.

Remove the nuts from the oven and allow them to cool before using or storing. To store, place them in an airtight container. They should keep well for a week or two.

Jordan's Spicy Sugar Cookies

Makes about 7 dozen 2½-inch cookies

As I worked on this book, my friend and the illustrator, Michel Stong, gave birth to a son, a beautiful dark-haired boy she named Jordan. When he was just a few weeks old, she had a welcoming party for him and I prepared the food. It was early spring, Valentine's Day, and beautiful wild mustard filled every undeveloped corner of Sonoma County. I decided to make some heart-shaped cookies, but to make them more interesting than the usual one-note sugar cookies we all know so well. These were a big hit—especially with the adults—and I now make them regularly, cutting them into shamrocks for St. Patrick's Day, bats and owls for Halloween, simple triangles or circles when there's no particular reason to make them other than their good, spicy depth of flavor.

1 1/2 cups butter, at room
  temperature
1 cup sugar
2 eggs
2 teaspoons good-quality
  vanilla extract
2 teaspoons finely ground
  black pepper
2 teaspoons hot mustard
  flour (or Colman's dry
  mustard)

2 teaspoons ground ginger
1/2 teaspoon cayenne
  pepper
2 to 4 teaspoons salt,
  preferably kosher
3 3/4 cups plus 2 table-
  spoons all-purpose flour
1 tablespoon water
Colored sugar (see Note)

Cream together the butter and sugar. Whisk together the
whole egg and the egg yolk of the second egg and reserve
the white. Add to the butter mixture and beat together well.
Mix in the vanilla, pepper, mustard, ginger, and half of the
cayenne pepper. Then stir in the salt. If you are using kosher
salt, add the entire 4 teaspoons. If you are using regular,
fine-grain salt, add 2 teaspoons and taste the mixture; it
should be slightly salty. Add as much of the remaining 2 teaspoons as necessary to obtain the proper balance, along
with as much of the remaining 1/4 teaspoon cayenne as desired for extra heat. Beat in the flour and divide the dough
into 4 equal portions. Wrap each in plastic wrap and chill
for at least 3 hours, or up to 3 days. Remove the dough from
the refrigerator 30 minutes before rolling it out.

On a floured surface, roll out each portion of dough
until it is 3/8 inch thick. Cut the dough into preferred shapes
and place the cookies on ungreased baking sheets. Mix together the reserved egg white and water, brush the surface
of the cookies with the mixture, and sprinkle a small amount

of colored sugar on top, in whatever pattern you prefer. The sugar does not need to cover the entire surface.

Bake the cookies in a 350°F oven for 7 to 9 minutes. They are done when they have just *barely* begun to color. Remove from the oven and cool on a rack. Store in airtight tins at room temperature.

Note: To make 1 cup colored sugar, place 1 cup of granulated or superfine sugar in a container with a lid. Add several drops of food coloring, close the container, and shake it until the sugar is evenly colored. Repeat the process for a more intense shade. Colored sugar will keep indefinitely in the pantry in a tightly sealed container.

Pots de Crème

Serves 8

These delicate custards have a rich complexity. Although the mustard itself disappears into the flavor of the whole, I believe it is the ingredient that draws all of the other elements together so beautifully.

1⅔ cups milk
1 vanilla bean, split and scraped
3 slices peeled fresh ginger
4 large (or 5 medium) egg yolks
⅓ cup sugar

1 teaspoon grated orange zest
2 tablespoons fresh squeezed orange juice
3 teaspoons hot mustard flour (or Colman's dry mustard)

Place the milk, vanilla bean, and ginger in a heavy saucepan and bring to a boil. Remove from the heat and let it sit, covered, for 15 to 30 minutes.

Whisk together the egg yolks and sugar, beating vigorously until the mixture is thick and lemon colored. Mix a paste of the orange zest, orange juice, and mustard flour and stir the paste into the egg yolk mixture.

Bring the milk to another boil and slowly drizzle in the egg yolk mixture, whisking constantly. Remove from the heat, let rest 5 minutes, and skim off any foam that forms on top. Strain the custard through a fine-mesh sieve, pour it into eight ½-cup ramekins (or other ovenproof containers), and set them in a baking dish that you have lined with wax paper. Place them in a 325°F oven, add enough boiling water to the dish so that it comes nearly halfway up the sides of the ramekins, and bake until surface is lightly golden and custard is set, for 30 to 35 minutes. Remove from the oven, let cool, and chill for at least 2 hours before serving.

 *Gingerbread*

Makes 1 9-inch square cake

No book about mustard or its history is complete without gingerbread, for which Dijon, France, is also famous. M. F. K. Fisher tells of how the aroma of pain d'épice *insinuated itself into every corner of Dijon, including the imaginations of all who smelled it. Although this recipe does not follow the traditional recipes of Dijon, which require rye flour and aging of the initial mixture for as long as several months (or years, she tells us in* Serve it Forth*), it does call for the addition of mustard flour, which the Dijon recipes also include.*

½ cup unsalted butter

½ cup brown sugar, firmly packed

1 egg

1 tablespoon grated fresh ginger

2 teaspoons orange zest, finely grated

2½ cups sifted all-purpose flour

1½ teaspoons baking soda

1 tablespoon hot mustard flour (or Colman's dry mustard)

1 teaspoon ground ginger

1 teaspoon ground cinnamon

½ teaspoon salt

½ cup light molasses

½ cup honey (see Note, page 174)

½ cup boiling water

½ cup orange juice, preferably fresh

Melt the butter in a heavy saucepan and then pour it into a large bowl and let cool slightly. Add the sugar, mix well, and stir in the egg, fresh ginger, and orange zest. Set the mixture aside. Sift together the all-purpose flour, baking soda, mustard flour, ground ginger, cinnamon, and salt. Combine the molasses, honey, boiling water, and orange juice.

Beat in the dry ingredients and the molasses mixture alternately to the butter mixture, about one third of each at a time.

Pour the gingerbread batter into a buttered, 9-inch square pan and bake at 350°F for about 1 hour, or until the center springs back when lightly touched. Take it out of the oven and place it on a rack to fully cool for 10 minutes before removing from the pan. Serve the gingerbread warm or at room temperature.

VARIATION:

Peel, core, and slice 2 pears and add them to the molasses mixture. Continue as the recipe directs. Traditional? No. Delicious? You bet.

Chia

Serves 4

Tea? For dessert? Certainly. This sweet and spicy tea is luscious and rich, and I find it quite satisfying as a light dessert. Serve it with sliced mangoes, Jordan's Spicy Sugar Cookies (page 199), Gingerbread (preceding recipe), or simply by itself.

2 cups milk
2 cups spring water
4 teaspoons black tea (see Note)
½ cup granulated sugar
1½-inch piece cinnamon stick
6 to 8 whole black peppercorns

1 teaspoon brown mustard seeds
3 whole cloves
¼ teaspoon cumin seeds
1 or 2 whole allspice berries
½ teaspoon ground nutmeg
½ teaspoon ground cardamom

In a heavy saucepan, combine the milk, water, sugar, and tea and bring the mixture to a boil. Remove from the heat, add all the spices, and let sit for 15 minutes. Bring to another boil, strain into a teapot or Thermos, and serve immediately. This tea can be made in advance, refrigerated, and reheated.
Note: Use a good, unscented strong black tea.

PART FOUR

Appendix

ACID As used in this book, any liquid that is acidic in nature, such as vinegar, lemon juice, or wine.

ALBA The scientific name of the group of *brassicas* that is commonly known as white mustard.

BÂTON The wooden handle on the top stone of a mustard quern (q.v.), used for turning the stone, which in turn grinds the mustard seed to a paste.

BRASSICA The scientific name of the genus of plants that includes the mustards.

CRUCIFERAE The scientific name of the family of plants that includes the cabbages, the mustards, the cresses, and horseradish. Member plants all have rounded four-petaled flowers that resemble a Maltese cross.

DRY MUSTARD A generic term that is generally understood to mean mustard flour (q.v.).

EXTRA VIRGIN OLIVE OIL Used to describe 100 percent olive oil with less than 1 percent oleic acid and with the characteristic full-bodied flavor of the olive. The best is from the first cold-pressing of superior olives, but much on the market today is refined olive oil with cold-pressed olive oil added for flavor.

GLUCOSIDE A member of a class of vegetable compounds that, in the presence of specific enzymes, releases glucose and another substance; in the case of mustard, this reaction creates its characteristic heat.

GROUND MUSTARD Ground whole mustard seeds, generally *Brassica alba*; has a coarse texture and speckled appearance. Not available to retail consumers; the majority is used by the meat industry as a seasoning in processed meats.

HIRTA The alternate scientific name of the group of white mustards more commonly called *Brassica alba*.

JUNCEA The scientific name of the group of brown mustards that includes Asian mustard and most mustards grown for their greens.

MUST The unfermented juice of grapes, on its way to being wine.

MUSTARD FLOUR Mustard seeds processed to remove the husk and the bran and then ground to produce a fine powder; available to retail consumers and often labeled as "dry mustard" or "dry mustard powder."

NEMOTODE A microscopic parasitic worm that infests certain soils; growing mustard can help control them.

QUATRE ÉPICES A classic seasoning traditionally composed of four ground spices: white pepper, cloves, ginger, and nutmeg, although chefs and spice manufacturers vary both the specific spices and their quantities to suit their personal preferences. Other spices that may be included are coriander, cardamom, allspice, and cinnamon.

QUERN In France, two large rough, heavy stones used to grind mustard seed to a fine paste; the top stone was turned by a wooden handle called a *bâton*. The quern was replaced by automatic machinery in the middle of the nineteenth century.

SINALBIN A glucoside present in white mustard seed (*Brassica hirta, Sinapis alba*) that disintegrates upon contact with water, precipitating the chemical reaction that produces the mustard's characteristic heat.

SINAPIS The alternate scientific name for white mustard, *Sinapis alba*, which has been generally abandoned in recent times in favor of *Brassica alba*. Some languages—Italian, German, and Greek, for example—developed their word for mustard from this Greek root.

SINIGRIN A glucoside present in brown (*Brassica juncea*) and black (*Brassica nigra, Sinapis nigra*) mustard seeds that disintegrates upon contact with water, precipitating the chemical reaction that produces the mustard's characteristic heat.

VERJUICE The juice of unripe grapes; it contains little or no sugar.

TASTING NOTES

Dijon & Dijon-Style Mustards

Source Country/State _____ Brand Name _____

Place of Purchase _____ Cost _____

Color/Appearance _____ Aroma _____

Texture _____ Consistency _____ Acidity _____

Taste _____ Balance _____ Finish _____

Notes _____

_____

Overall Opinion _____ Will Purchase Again _____

Source Country/State _____ Brand Name _____

Place of Purchase _____ Cost _____

Color/Appearance _____ Aroma _____

Texture _____ Consistency _____ Acidity _____

Taste _____ Balance _____ Finish _____

Notes _____

_____

Overall Opinion _____ Will Purchase Again _____

Source Country/State _____ Brand Name _____

Place of Purchase _____ Cost _____

Color/Appearance _____ Aroma _____

Texture _____ Consistency _____ Acidity _____

Taste _____ Balance _____ Finish _____

Notes _____

_____

Overall Opinion _____ Will Purchase Again _____

Coarse-Grain Mustards

Source Country/State _____ Brand Name _____
Place of Purchase _____ Cost _____
Color/Appearance _____ Aroma _____
Texture _____ Bite _____ Consistency _____ Acidity _____
Taste _____ Balance _____ Finish _____
Ingredients _____
Notes _____
Overall Opinion _____ Will Purchase Again _____

Source Country/State _____ Brand Name _____
Place of Purchase _____ Cost _____
Color/Appearance _____ Aroma _____
Texture _____ Bite _____ Consistency _____ Acidity _____
Taste _____ Balance _____ Finish _____
Ingredients _____
Notes _____
Overall Opinion _____ Will Purchase Again _____

Source Country/State _____ Brand Name _____
Place of Purchase _____ Cost _____
Color/Appearance _____ Aroma _____
Texture _____ Bite _____ Consistency _____ Acidity _____
Taste _____ Balance _____ Finish _____
Ingredients _____
Notes _____
Overall Opinion _____ Will Purchase Again _____

Flavored Mustards & Other Mustards

Source Country/State _____ Brand Name _____
Place of Purchase _____ Cost _____
Color/Appearance _____ Aroma _____
Texture _____ Consistency _____ Acidity _____
Taste of flavoring _____ Balance _____ Finish _____
Ingredients _____
Notes _____
Overall Opinion _____ Will Purchase Again _____

Source Country/State _____ Brand Name _____
Place of Purchase _____ Cost _____
Color/Appearance _____ Aroma _____
Texture _____ Consistency _____ Acidity _____
Taste of flavoring _____ Balance _____ Finish _____
Ingredients _____
Notes _____
Overall Opinion _____ Will Purchase Again _____

Source Country/State _____ Brand Name _____
Place of Purchase _____ Cost _____
Color/Appearance _____ Aroma _____
Texture _____ Consistency _____ Acidity _____
Taste of flavoring _____ Balance _____ Finish _____
Ingredients _____
Notes _____
Overall Opinion _____ Will Purchase Again _____

BIBLIOGRAPHY

Aresty, Esther B. *The Delectable Past.* New York: Bobbs-Merrill, 1978.

Behr, Edward. *The Artful Eater.* New York: Atlantic Monthly Press, 1992.

Brabazon, James. *Dorothy L. Sayers.* New York: Avon Books, 1981.

Brillat-Savarin, Jean Anthelme. *The Physiology of Taste.* Translated by M. F. K. Fisher. New York: Harvest Books, 1978.

Chapman, Robert L., Ph.D., ed. *New Dictionary of American Slang.* New York: Harper and Row, 1986.

Colman, Louis, ed. and trans. *Alexandre Dumas' Dictionary of Cuisine.* London: Spring Books, 1964.

Fisher, M. F. K. *The Art of Eating.* New York: Macmillan, 1990.

Gray, Patience. *Honey from a Weed.* San Francisco: North Point Press, 1990.

Hazen, Janet. *Mustard.* San Francisco: Chronicle Books, 1993.

Hopley, Claire. *Making & Using Mustards.* Pownal, Vt.: Storey Communications, 1991.

Kamman, Madeleine. *In Madeleine's Kitchen.* New York: Atheneum, 1984.

———. *The Making of a Cook.* New York: Atheneum, 1971.

Lake, Mark, and Judy Ridgway. *Oils, Vinegars & Seasonings.* New York: Simon and Schuster, 1989.

Lang, Jenifer Harvey. *Tastings.* New York: Crown, 1986.

Man, Rosamond, and Robin Weir. *The Compleat Mustard.* London: Constable and Company, 1988.

McGee, Harold. *On Food and Cooking.* New York: Charles Scribner's Sons, 1984.

————. *The Curious Cook*. San Francisco: North Point Press, 1990.

Sawyer, Helene. *Gourmet Mustards: How to Make Them and Cook with Them*. Lake Oswego, Ore.: Culinary Arts, 1990.

Plageman, Catherine, and M. F. K. Fisher. *Fine Preserving*. Reading, Mass.: Aris Books/Addison-Wesley, 1986.

Roach, Jill, and Sheldon Greenberg, producers. *Mustard: The Spice of Nations*. Evanston, Ill.: Beacon Films, Inc., 1983.

Root, Waverly. *The Food of France*. New York: Alfred A. Knopf, 1970.

Scully, Virginia. *A Treasury of American Indian Herbs*. New York: Crown Publishers, 1970.

Simetti, Mary Taylor. *Pomp and Sustenance*. New York: Alfred A. Knopf, 1989.

Shields, John. *The Chesapeake Bay Crab Cookbook*. Reading, Mass.: Aris Books/Addison-Wesley, 1990.

Stone, Sally, and Martin Stone. *The Mustard Cookbook*. New York: Avon Books, 1981.

Tannahill, Reay. *Food in History*. New York: Stein and Day, 1973.

Tarantino, Jim. *Marinades*. Freedom, Calif.: The Crossing Press, 1992.

Whealy, Kent. *Garden Seed Inventory*, 3rd ed. Decorah, Iowa: Seed Saver Publications, 1992.

Wolfe, Linda. *The Literary Gourmet*. New York: Harmony Books, 1985.

RESOURCES

Bornibus
60 boulevard de la Villette
Paris, France

Grey Poupon
rue de la Liberté
Dijon, France

Joe Matos Cheese Factory
3669 Llano Road
Santa Rosa, CA 95407
(707) 584-5283
St. George Cheese, mail order

Kermit Lynch Wine Merchant
1605 San Pablo Avenue
Berkeley, CA 94702-1317
(510) 524-1524

Mount Horeb Mustard
   Museum
109 East Main Street
Mount Horeb, WI 53572
(608) 437-3986

The Proper Mustard
P.O. Box 468
Mount Horeb, WI 53572
Official newsletter of the
   Mount Horeb Mustard
   Museum

Seed Savers Exchange
Kent Whealy, Director
Rural Route 3, Box 239
Decorah, IA 52101

INDEX

Naigeon, Jean, 21

Olives
   in mustard seed and anchovy
      marinade, 59–60
   in olive-anchovy mustard, 180
   with potato salad, Italian
      salami, and arugula,
      156–157
   in three-olive mustard, 179–180
Omelets, 57
Onions
   with grilled sausages and
      assorted mustards,
      121–122
   with oranges, red peppers, and
      mustard greens, 148–149
   red, in rib-eye steak with
      fennel, cucumbers, and
      horseradish-mustard
      sauce, 113–114
   in sauce, 122–123
Oranges
   with onions, red peppers, and
      mustard greens, 148–149
   in orange mustard cream, 187
   in orange-mustard sauce,
      125–127
   slices, seared, with mustard and
      arugula, 161–162
Oriental mustard, 50
Orzo, in chicken breasts
    marinated in mustard oil,
    104–105

Pasta
   angel hair, in composed salad
      with chicken and
      preserved lemons, 152–154

Pasta (*Cont.*)
   flan salad with romaine
      lettuce and Caesar-style
      dressing, 149–152
   linguine with salmon, red
      peppers, and broccoli
      rabe, 78–79
   macaroni and cheese with
      mustard greens, 80–81
   macaroni salad, 57
Pear sauce, Dijon, 192
Pecans, spicy toasted,
    198–199
Peppers, red
   in linguine with salmon and
      broccoli rabe, 78–79
   with oranges, onions, and
      mustard greens,
      148–149
Pickle(s), mustard, 194–196
Pickled mustard root, 46, 50
Plum-mustard sauce, 190–191
Polenta
   with chicken and broccoli
      rabe, 102–103
   with sausages, apples, and
      mustard greens,
      100–102
Pommery mustard, 24
Pork
   ham with red-eye gravy,
      134–135
   loin
      with apricot-mustard glaze,
         123–125
      in mustard crust with
         orange-mustard sauce,
         125–127
   See also Sausage